Future Proofing your life: A Guide for GenZ to Navigate Jobs, Skills, and Life's Curveballs

Guy Ellis

To Cam.

You are my inspiration for writing this book.

© Copyright 2024 - All rights reserved.

Legal Notice:

This book is copyright protected. It is only for personal use. You cannot amend, distribute, sell, use, quote or paraphrase any part, or the content within this book, without the consent of the author or publisher.

Disclaimer Notice:

Please note the information contained within this document is for educational and entertainment purposes only. All effort has been executed to present accurate, up to date, reliable, complete information. No warranties of any kind are declared or implied. Readers acknowledge that the author is not engaged in the rendering of legal or professional advice. The content within this book has been derived from various sources. Please consult a licensed professional before attempting any techniques outlined in this book.

By reading this document, the reader agrees that under no circumstances is the author responsible for any losses, direct or indirect, that are incurred as a result of the use of the information contained within this document, including, but not limited to, errors, omissions, or inaccuracies.

Contents

Acknowledgements:..10

Introduction:..11

Part 1: Understanding Yourself and Your Career Path................13

Chapter 1: Who Are You (Really)?..15

    Understanding Your Values...16

    Understanding Your Strengths..16

    Your Career Doesn't Have to Be a Straight Line.............17

    Chapter 1 Summary..18

Chapter 2: What Do You Really Want?..................................19

    Listening to Yourself (Not Everyone Else).....................20

    Balancing Passion with Practicality.................................20

    You Don't Have to Know Everything Right Now...........21

    Chapter 2 Summary..22

Chapter 3: Taking the Pressure Off..23

    The Myth of "Having It All Figured Out".......................24

    The Power of Being a "Late Bloomer"............................25

    Your First Job Isn't Your Last Job.....................................26

    Embracing Mistakes and Setbacks..................................26

    Chapter 3 Summary..27

Part 1 Summary: Understanding Yourself and Your Career Path........29

    Looking Ahead: What's Next?..29

Part 2: Practical Steps to Building Your Career............................31

Chapter 4: How to Figure Out What You're Good At...........32

- Why Skills Matter (And How to Build Them)..................32
- Why Trying Different Jobs Helps..................33
- The Power of Building Skills Outside of Work..................34
- Why Skills Give You Confidence..................35
- Chapter 4 Summary..................35

Chapter 5: Skills That Matter (and How to Get Them)..................36
- Why Skills Are the Currency of the Job Market..................36
- Hard Skills: The Technical Side of Things..................36
- Soft Skills: The Game Changers..................37
- How to Build the Skills You Need..................38
- Why Skill-Building is a Lifelong Journey..................39
- Chapter 5 Summary..................39

Chapter 6: Why Making Mistakes is Part of the Plan..................41
- The Fear of Failure..................41
- How to Learn from Mistakes..................42
- Why Mistakes Build Resilience..................43
- Why Perfection Isn't the Goal..................44
- Chapter 6 Summary..................44

Chapter 7: Building Confidence Without Faking It..................45
- Why Confidence Matters..................45
- Why Preparation Builds Confidence..................46
- Confidence Without Perfection..................47
- How to Handle Imposter Syndrome..................47
- Confidence Comes From Action..................48
- Chapter 7 Summary..................49

Part 2 Summary: Practical Steps to Building Your Career..................................50
    Looking Ahead: What's Next?..................................51
Part 3 Introduction: Landing the Job (Without Losing Your Mind)................51
Chapter 8: How to Write a CV That Gets Noticed..................................53
    What Your CV Really Says About You..................................53
    The Key Components of a Great CV..................................53
    How to Tailor Your CV for Each Job..................................55
    Design and Layout: Keep It Simple..................................56
    Why Your CV is Only the Beginning..................................56
    Chapter 8 Summary..................................56
Chapter 9: Acing the Interview..................................58
    Why Preparation is Key..................................58
    Common Interview Questions and How to Answer Them..................59
    Virtual Interviews: What's Different?..................................61
    Asking Questions: The Interview Goes Both Ways..................................62
    Chapter 9 Summary..................................63
Chapter 10: Networking Without Feeling Awkward..................................64
    Why Networking Matters..................................64
    How to Network (Without Feeling Awkward)..................................65
    In-Person Networking: Making It Less Awkward..................................66
    Chapter 10 Summary..................................68
Part 3 Summary: Landing the Job..................................69
    What's Next?..................................69
Part 4 Introduction: Thriving in the Workplace (And Beyond)..................70
Chapter 11: Starting Your First Job (And Doing It Well)..................................71

- Why the First Few Weeks Matter 71
- How to Make a Great First Impression 72
- Navigating Workplace Culture 74
- The Importance of Asking for Feedback 75
- Chapter 11 Summary 75

Chapter 12: Mastering Workplace Social Skills and Etiquette 77
- Workplace Etiquette 101 77
- Navigating Social Dynamics 78
- Fitting In While Staying Authentic 79
- Handling Office Politics 80
- Receiving and Using Feedback 80
- Chapter 12 Summary 81

Chapter 13: How to Keep Growing in Your Career 82
- Why Career Growth is Important 82
- How to Keep Growing in Your Career 83
- How to Track Your Growth 84
- The Power of Mentorship 85
- Chapter 13 Summary 86

Chapter 14: Finding Balance and Avoiding Burnout 88
- Why Work-Life Balance is Essential 88
- How to Set Boundaries at Work 89
- Recognising the Signs of Burnout 90
- Chapter 14 Summary 92

Part 4 Summary: Thriving in the Workplace (And Beyond) 93
- Looking Ahead: What's Next? 94

Part 5 Introduction: Career Change or Curveball? That's Okay Too!...........95

Chapter 15: When You Want to Change Your Career (And Don't Know How)..97

    How to Know When It's Time for a Change............................97

    How to Make a Career Change (Without Starting Over)......................99

    How to Overcome the Fear of Change..................................100

    Chapter 15 Summary..101

Chapter 16: Handling Career Curveballs (And Bouncing Back)................101

    How to Manage Career Setbacks..102

    How to Pivot After a Job Loss...103

    How to Stay Resilient in Times of Uncertainty......................104

    Chapter 16 Summary..105

Chapter 17: The Future of Work...106

    Embrace Lifelong Learning..106

    Technology and Automation: A Friend, Not a Foe..............107

    Remote Work and Flexibility: The New Normal..................107

    Building Your Network in the Future of Work....................108

    Preparing for Multiple Career Changes..............................109

Chapter 17 Summary...109

Part 5 Summary: Career Change or Curveball? That's Okay Too!...............111

    Looking Ahead: What's Next?..111

Conclusion: Bringing It All Home..112

    Remember, It's a Journey, Not a Race................................112

    Building Your Career, Step by Step.....................................112

    Your Career, Your Way...113

 Looking Ahead..114

Hints and Tips..115

 Part 1: Understanding Yourself and Your Career Path........................115

 Part 2: Practical Steps to Building Your Career....................................116

 Part 3: Landing the Job..117

 Part 4: Thriving in the Workplace (And Beyond)..................................118

 Part 5: Career Change or Curveball? That's Okay Too!........................120

Resources..122

 Part 1: Understanding Yourself and Your Career Path........................122

 Part 2: Practical Steps to Building Your Career....................................122

 Part 3: Landing the Job..123

 Part 4: Thriving in the Workplace (And Beyond)..................................124

 Part 5: Career Change or Curveball? That's Okay Too!........................125

About the Author- Guy Ellis..126

Acknowledgements:

This book has been many years in the making and a number of people have helped me along the way.

Without Graham Scott, a close friend, who I co-authored a book on how organisations can attract, motivate and retain young people (Gen Z), there would be no underlying research.

Without Chris O'Brien, another close friend with whom I ran a business with, there would not have been the many years of my blogs, whitepapers and articles about careers and related topics.

And my children, newly minted from University, and the young adults of friends, with whom I have tried to help make sense of their career options.

I'd also like to thank the team at the London School of Digital Business – in particular Shrushti and Vaibhav. Their support and advice have been invaluable.

And with the help of ChatGPT, I was able to bring the many tens of thousands of words that I have written from dozens of sources into one book. Such is the power of technology, but also a demonstration that we all need to keep learning, be open to new ways of doing things and never assume that our current career is our last one.

Introduction

Welcome. If you've picked up this book, you're probably feeling a little unsure about the future. You might be wondering what career you want, how to even get started, or if it's okay that you don't have it all figured out yet. Well, take a deep breath—you're in the right place, and you're not alone.

Here's the truth: nobody has it all sorted out, especially not in their late teens or twenties. Some people act like they do, but behind that confidence is someone who's learning and making it up as they go along—just like you. The good news? That's perfectly okay. In fact, it's normal.

This book isn't here to give you a magic formula or tell you exactly what to do with your life. Spoiler alert: that doesn't exist. Instead, I'm here to help you figure out a few things for yourself. Think of me as your kindly uncle, the one who'll give you the honest truth but also cheer you on every step of the way. I want you to succeed, but I'm not going to sugarcoat things either—life can be tough, and careers can be confusing. But, with a little guidance, some practical steps, and a lot of self-belief, you'll get there.

Now, let's take a moment to talk about something important: your mental health. You've probably heard a lot about it by now, and rightly so—taking care of your mind is just as important as looking after your body. The world can be overwhelming, and figuring out your career on top of everything else can feel like a lot. So yes, it's crucial to take care of yourself, give yourself breaks, and not be too hard on yourself when things feel heavy.

But, here's the thing. Life—and your career—will push you out of your comfort zone. In fact, that's where real growth happens. It's okay to feel scared or uncertain, but it's important to step forward anyway. That's how you build resilience—the ability to bounce back when things don't go as planned, to keep going even when it's hard. Resilience isn't about being tough all the time; it's about knowing you can handle challenges when they come your way. And trust me, they will come. But so will the opportunities.

We're going to find a balance between recognising when you need to rest and when it's time to push yourself a little further. After all, you're building the skills now that will carry you through not just your first job, but your whole life. Part of that is learning how to manage stress, how to adapt when things change, and how to keep moving forward, even when things feel uncertain.

It's okay to make mistakes. In fact, I encourage it. Mistakes are how we grow, how we figure out what works and what doesn't. They're not something to be ashamed of—they're something to learn from. And if there's one thing I want you to remember as you go through this book, it's this: your career, and your life, are your own. You get to shape them, change them, and grow with them. There's no one "right" way to do it.

So let's take this journey together. I'll give you the tools, the advice, and maybe even a few laughs along the way. All you need to bring is an open mind, a willingness to learn, and the belief that you *can* do this—even when it feels like you can't.

Ready? Let's go.

Part 1: Understanding Yourself and Your Career Path

Before we get into the practical steps of job hunting, CV writing, and interviews, let's take a moment to focus on the most important thing—you.

When it comes to choosing a career, most people jump straight into the "what" and "how" without taking the time to figure out the "why." But here's the thing: your career is about more than just earning a pay check. It's about finding work that feels meaningful, something that aligns with your values, strengths, and interests. That's why we're starting with some self-reflection.

In this part of the book, we're going to explore *who* you are and *what* you really want. Because when you understand yourself better, you can make decisions that not only lead to success but also fulfilment.

This section isn't about having everything figured out right away—it's about starting the journey of discovery. You'll learn to listen to your inner voice, sort through all the noise from other people's expectations, and understand what truly excites and drives you. You'll also see that it's okay if you don't have a straight path mapped out just yet. Life isn't linear, and your career doesn't need to be either.

We're going to dig into some key questions:

- What are your values? What do you care about, and how do those values translate into your work?
- What are your strengths? What are you naturally good at, and how can those talents shape your career?
- And perhaps the hardest question: What do you *really* want? Not what others want for you, but what *you* want.

We'll also talk about the pressure to have it all figured out by a certain age and why it's perfectly okay if you're still finding your way. This part of the book is all about taking that pressure off, embracing mistakes as part of the learning process, and building the resilience you'll need to navigate your career and life.

Ready to dive in? Let's start by figuring out *who* you are—because that's the foundation for everything that comes next.

Chapter 1: Who Are You (Really)?

Alright, let's start with a big question: *Who are you?* Don't worry—I'm not expecting you to have some deep, philosophical answer right away. Most people spend years figuring this out, and even then, they don't have all the answers. But when it comes to your career, taking the time to understand yourself is the first step in figuring out where you might want to go.

The more you understand what makes you tick, the easier it becomes to make decisions about your future. So let's break this down into more practical steps.

Exercise 1: Yesterday, Today, and Tomorrow

Here's a simple exercise to help you reflect on how your past, present, and future shape who you are. Grab a piece of paper, divide it into three sections—Yesterday, Today, and Tomorrow—and jot down your thoughts on the following:

- **Yesterday:** What experiences, people, or events have shaped who you are? Think about both good and bad experiences—everything counts. How have they influenced your strengths, weaknesses, and values?
- **Today:** What do you care about right now? What's important to you in your life and work? Are there activities or roles where you feel like you're thriving?
- **Tomorrow:** What excites or scares you about the future? What would you like to achieve, or what kinds of things do you see yourself doing?

This exercise helps you reflect on how your past has influenced your present and where you might want to go in the future. It's not about having all the answers—it's about noticing patterns and paying attention to what makes you feel energised or curious.

Understanding Your Values

Values are the things that matter most to you. They're like the compass that guides your decisions, whether you realise it or not. Some people value creativity, others crave stability. Some love a challenge, while others value connection and relationships. Knowing your core values helps you figure out what kind of work will be meaningful and fulfilling for you.

Let's try another exercise to help you explore your values.

Exercise 2: Your Values and Purpose

Answer the following questions—go with your gut instinct:

- What motivates me to get up in the morning?
- What am I doing when I feel happiest or most energised?
- What frustrates or bothers me deeply in life?
- Why do I do the work I do (or why would I like to do certain types of work)?
- When have I felt the proudest of myself or fulfilled in life?

Now, look over your answers and try to spot any recurring themes. These are likely connected to your core values. For example, if you feel proud when you help others, you might value service and making a difference. If you feel energised when solving problems, creativity or intellectual challenge might be core values.

Understanding Your Strengths

Knowing what you're good at is another key part of figuring out your career path. Your strengths are not just your technical skills (like coding or writing)—they also include your natural talents, like communication, empathy, or problem-solving.

Exercise 3: The SOAR Analysis

The SOAR analysis is a simple but effective exercise to help you recognise your strengths and opportunities. Grab your notebook again, and under each of the following headings, write down a few thoughts:

- **S (Strengths):** What are you naturally good at? What do people compliment you on? What are the things that feel easy for you but might seem difficult to others?
- **O (Opportunities):** What opportunities are out there for you to explore, whether in terms of skills, learning, or career options?
- **A (Aspirations):** What do you want to achieve? What kind of career or role do you see yourself in?
- **R (Results):** What results do you want from your efforts? How will you measure success in your life and career?

This exercise isn't about having all the answers right now—it's about starting the process of self-discovery for success and understanding what you're naturally good at and how that can shape your career choices.

Your Career Doesn't Have to Be a Straight Line

Here's a key takeaway: your career doesn't have to follow a straight path. It's normal to zigzag, try new things, and even start over. Each job or experience you have helps you build skills and knowledge, and all of those pieces come together to shape your future.

People often worry that they have to make one big, perfect career choice, but that's not how it works anymore. The most successful people are often those who've tried a few different things, learned from their experiences, and figured out what works for them over time.

So, don't stress if you don't have a clear, defined path just yet. The key is to keep moving forward, exploring, and learning more about yourself along the way.

Chapter 1 Summary

To summarise:

- Start by reflecting on your past, present, and future. Notice patterns in what excites you and what feels meaningful.
- Understand your values—they are your compass in making decisions about your life and career.
- Take stock of your strengths and natural talents. Use exercises like SOAR to clarify what you're good at and what opportunities might be out there.
- Remember, your career path will likely zigzag. The important thing is to keep exploring, learning, and adjusting as you go.

Let's move on to the next chapter, where we'll dive deeper into what you really want—and how to balance that with practicality.

Chapter 2: What Do You Really Want?

Now that we've started exploring who you are, let's tackle another big question: *What do you really want?* This isn't just about figuring out a job title or career path—it's about understanding what you want from life and how your work can fit into that bigger picture.

You might feel pressure from all sides—parents, friends, society—to make decisions about your future. But here's the thing: the person who's going to live your life is *you*. That means it's important to figure out what will make *you* feel fulfilled, excited, and satisfied in your work, not just what will please others.

Let's break it down, one step at a time, so you can start uncovering what you really want.

Exercise 1: What's Important to You?

This first exercise will help you dig deeper into your personal priorities and what you want from your work. Grab your notebook, and think about the following questions:

- What activities make you feel excited or energised?
- What kind of lifestyle do you want? Do you value flexibility and free time, or are you driven by the idea of hard work and achievement?
- When you think about your future, what kind of impact do you want to make in the world?
- If you could design your ideal workday, what would it look like? What kind of environment would you be in?

The goal here is to get a clearer sense of what truly matters to you. Are you someone who wants to help others, or do you thrive on solving complex problems? Do you crave creativity, or are you more focused on stability and security? These insights will help with career planning for beginners as you reflect on what's truly important.

This exercise is about noticing what you're drawn to. Pay attention to the things that feel important to *you*—not what others expect or want.

Listening to Yourself (Not Everyone Else)

It's easy to let other people's expectations shape your decisions, whether it's the pressure to enter a high-paying field or the need to follow in your family's footsteps. But remember: it's *your* life. While it's fine to take advice from others, the final decision has to feel right to *you*.

Let's explore how to navigate the noise of other people's expectations while tuning into your own desires.

Exercise 2: The "Should vs. Want" List

One way to start sorting through the noise is to create a "Should vs. Want" list. On one side of a piece of paper, write down all the things you feel like you "should" do—things others have told you, or expectations you feel from society. On the other side, write down the things you actually *want* to do.

Here are a few prompts to help:

- What careers or paths do others expect from you?
- What career paths actually interest you, even if they don't align with others' expectations?
- What do you feel like you should do because it's "practical" or "safe," and what would you pursue if there were no limits?

This exercise is about getting clarity on what influences your decisions. Are you choosing certain paths because you think you *should*? What's on the "want" side, and how can you explore those interests without feeling guilty?

Balancing Passion with Practicality

Here's where things can get tricky. It's great to have passion, but what if your passion doesn't seem practical? A lot of people feel stuck when their interests don't line up with what seems like a stable or secure career path. But here's the thing: you don't have to choose between passion and practicality—you can blend the two.

Let's explore how you can pursue your interests while still being realistic about your goals.

Exercise 3: The Ideal Job Description

This exercise from the *Career Clarity Handbook* helps you think about what your ideal job might look like. Don't worry about how realistic it is right now—this is about exploring your dreams.

Write down the answers to these prompts:

- What would your perfect job be like? Think about tasks, responsibilities, and the people you'd work with.
- What kind of company or environment would you want to work in (big corporate, startup, creative space)?
- What skills and talents would you use in this role?
- How would this job make you feel at the end of the day—fulfilled, challenged, creative?

After completing this exercise, look over your answers and reflect on them. What common themes do you notice? Are there parts of this ideal job that you could incorporate into a real-world role? Sometimes, you can find practical ways to use your passions—maybe you love music, but instead of being a musician, you can work in music production or marketing for artists. The key is finding ways to weave your interests into your career while balancing practicality.

You Don't Have to Know Everything Right Now

The idea that you need to have your whole life planned out in your twenties is outdated. Sure, it might seem like everyone else has it figured out but trust me—most people are figuring things out as they go. Your twenties are a time for exploration, experimentation, and learning. You don't need to know *exactly* what you want right now. What's more important is that you stay curious, open to new experiences, and ready to learn from whatever comes your way.

Here's an exercise to help ease some of that pressure.

Exercise 4: Thinking Ahead (Without Overthinking)

We're going to map out a few possible futures for yourself. This isn't about locking in a single career path—it's about seeing what options are out there and how they align with your interests and values.

Think of three different futures for yourself:

- **Safe and Comfortable:** What would your career look like if you chose something practical and stable? What kind of work would you be doing? How would that make you feel?
- **Dream Big:** What would your ideal, no-holds-barred future look like? If you didn't have to worry about money or expectations, what would you do?
- **Somewhere in Between:** What could a middle ground look like, combining some practicality with passion? How can you balance financial security with work that excites and fulfils you?

By thinking of multiple paths, you'll realise that there's no single "right" answer. You're not stuck with just one option, and your career will evolve over time. The goal is to find a path that excites you, even if it's not the perfect mix of passion and practicality right away.

Chapter 2 Summary

Here's what we've covered:

- You get to decide what's important to you, not what others expect.

- Balancing passion with practicality is key—there's no need to choose one over the other.
- It's okay if you don't have everything figured out yet. Your career will evolve, and it's about staying curious and open to possibilities.

In the next chapter, we'll talk about taking the pressure off and embracing the idea that it's okay not to have all the answers right now. We'll explore why the journey is just as important as the destination, and how to build resilience along the way.

Chapter 3: Taking the Pressure Off

We've all felt it—that pressure to "figure it all out" by a certain age. Social media doesn't help, with everyone showing off their best moments, making it seem like they've got life all sorted. But here's the truth: most people don't. The sooner you realise that, the easier it will be to take the pressure off yourself.

In this chapter, we'll focus on understanding that your career (and life!) doesn't have to follow a strict timeline. We'll also explore how to deal with setbacks, why it's okay to make mistakes, and how to build resilience for the long run.

The Myth of "Having It All Figured Out"

There's this myth that you're supposed to have your career path figured out by your early twenties. Society, and even some well-meaning people around you, might say, "By 25, you should have a stable job, a plan, and know exactly where you're heading." But the reality is, that's just not how life works.

Most people spend years exploring different paths, changing jobs, and discovering what really fulfils them. Many successful people didn't start their dream careers until later in life. So, if you're feeling like you're behind, relax—you're right on track.

Exercise 1: Reframing the Timeline

Let's challenge this idea of needing to "have it all together" by a certain age. In this exercise, you'll map out a more flexible and realistic career timeline for yourself.

- **Age 25:** What do you hope to learn or explore by this age? Focus on skills, experiences, and personal growth, not necessarily a specific job title.

- **Age 30:** What would you like to be doing in your career or personal life by 30? Again, think about the kind of work or life balance you'd want, not just external markers of success.
- **Beyond 30:** What long-term goals or dreams do you have for your future? These could be career-related or personal, such as traveling, learning new skills, or starting a passion project.

The goal here is to see your career and life as an evolving journey, not a sprint to a finish line. Your twenties are for exploration, trying new things, and figuring out what fits. You have time.

The Power of Being a "Late Bloomer"

You've probably heard stories of people who seem to have it all figured out early in life—starting successful businesses at 23 or landing their dream job right after graduation. But for every one of those stories, there are many more of people who took longer to find their path—and that's okay.

Let's talk about being a "late bloomer." In reality, there's no such thing as being late to your own life. Whether you figure things out at 25, 35, or even 50, the journey is just as important as the destination. The skills and experiences you gain along the way shape you into who you're meant to be.

Exercise 2: Celebrating Late Bloomers

To take the pressure off yourself, it can help to see real-world examples of people who found success later in life. Take a moment to research at least three "late bloomers"—people who made a major career switch or found success after 30 or even later. Write down their stories and reflect on how they stayed resilient and open to change.

Some examples:

- Vera Wang didn't design her first dress until she was 40.
- J.K. Rowling was in her 30s, a single mother, and living on benefits before publishing *Harry Potter*.

- Colonel Sanders started KFC in his 60s after a string of failed ventures.

By looking at their stories, you'll realise that success isn't about when you start—it's about staying persistent, learning, and growing over time.

Your First Job Isn't Your Last Job

One of the biggest misconceptions is that your first job defines your whole career. That's not true at all. Think of your first job as a learning experience—a stepping stone, not a final destination.

You might not land your dream job right away, and that's okay. What's more important is that you're building skills, getting experience, and figuring out what you like (and don't like). Each role you take helps you understand what you want more of, and what to avoid.

Exercise 3: The Career Stepping Stones

Here's an exercise to help you see your career as a series of stepping stones, each one building on the last.

- **Look at Your Current (or First) Job:** What skills or experiences are you gaining from this role? What are you learning, even if it's not your dream job?
- **Next Step:** Based on your current job, what would you want to do next? What skills or experiences do you want to build on in your next role?
- **Longer-Term:** Where do you see yourself heading in the next few years? Not a specific title, but what kind of work excites you, or what kind of projects would you love to take on?

By thinking of your career as a journey, with each job leading to the next, you take the pressure off needing to land the "perfect" job right away. Each step counts.

Embracing Mistakes and Setbacks

Here's something nobody tells you enough: mistakes are part of the process. You're going to make them, and that's completely normal. In fact, it's necessary. Mistakes teach you what works, what doesn't, and where you need to grow. Without them, there's no learning.

The same goes for setbacks. Maybe you don't land a job you wanted, or you feel like you're in the wrong role. That doesn't mean you've failed. It means you're learning more about what fits you and what doesn't.

Exercise 4: The Resilience Reflection

Think back to a time when something didn't go as planned. Maybe it was a job application that didn't work out, or a project that didn't go well. Reflect on the following:

- What did you learn from that experience?
- How did it help you grow, even if it felt difficult at the time?
- How can you use that experience to make better decisions in the future?

Building resilience is about learning to bounce back from setbacks, not avoiding them. The more you can reflect on what you've learned, the better equipped you'll be for the future.

Chapter 3 Summary

To sum up:

- You don't need to have it all figured out right now. Most people are still learning and growing well into their thirties and beyond.
- There's power in being a "late bloomer"—your career and life are on *your* timeline.
- Your first job is just the beginning. Each role is a stepping stone to the next.

- Mistakes and setbacks are part of the journey. They help you build resilience and shape your path forward.

As we move forward, remember to give yourself space to learn, grow, and make mistakes. The journey is what matters, not just the destination. Next, we'll dive into practical steps to figure out what skills you need and how to start building them.

Part 1 Summary: Understanding Yourself and Your Career Path

So, here we are. You've taken some important first steps in understanding who you are and where you might want to go in life. Figuring out your career path isn't about having all the answers right away—it's about exploring, learning, and staying open to change. Let's recap the key takeaways from these first few chapters:

- **Who You Are Matters**

    In Chapter 1, we talked about understanding your values, strengths, and past experiences. Knowing what drives you is the foundation for making decisions about your future. Through exercises like "Yesterday, Today, and Tomorrow" and the SOAR analysis, you've begun the process of identifying what's important to you and what you're naturally good at.

- **Listen to Yourself, Not Everyone Else**

    Chapter 2 was all about tuning in to your own desires rather than living by others' expectations. Balancing passion with practicality is key, but ultimately, this is *your* life and career. We explored tools like the "Should vs. Want" list and the "Ideal Job Description" exercise to help you clarify what excites you and what feels right for you.

- **Take the Pressure Off**

    In Chapter 3, we broke down the myth that you need to have it all figured out by a certain age. Life—and your career—is a journey, not a race. Being a "late bloomer" is okay, and your first job is just a stepping stone. We focused on resilience, learning from mistakes, and embracing the idea that setbacks are part of growth.

Looking Ahead: What's Next?

Now that you've done some important self-reflection, we're ready to get practical. In the next part of the book, we'll dive into actionable steps for building your career. From figuring out what skills you need to crafting a standout CV, preparing for interviews, and navigating your first job, we're going to break it all down into manageable steps.

Remember, it's not about rushing to the finish line—it's about making progress, one step at a time.

So take a deep breath. You've got this. Let's keep going.

Part 2: Practical Steps to Building Your Career

Alright, now that we've done some important self-reflection and started understanding what makes you tick, it's time to shift gears. In this part of the book, we're getting practical. We're going to focus on the *how*—how to turn what you've learned about yourself into real, actionable steps for building your career.

Think of Part 2 as your career toolkit. We'll cover the basics you need to start moving forward:

- How to discover and build the skills that matter most to employers.
- How to write a standout CV that gets you noticed.
- How to prepare for interviews and show up as your best, most confident self.

But more than that, we'll talk about how to navigate the job search without losing your mind. The process can be stressful—there's no doubt about that. So, I'm going to give you some tools to help make it a little easier, and maybe even a bit fun (yes, fun!). From networking without feeling awkward to mastering virtual interviews, you'll find practical tips here that you can use right away.

Remember, you don't have to do everything perfectly. This is all about learning as you go, building confidence, and realising that every step you take is moving you closer to where you want to be. The goal isn't to rush to the finish line, but to start building a foundation that will support you throughout your career.

Whether you're just starting out or already working and looking for your next move, these chapters will give you the tools and insights to take that next step with confidence.

So, let's dive in and start making things happen!

Chapter 4: How to Figure Out What You're Good At

By now, you've probably thought a lot about who you are, your values, and what matters to you. That's great, but now we're moving into something equally important: figuring out what you're *good at*. The truth is, we all have strengths—natural talents that we might not even realise we have because they come so easily. This chapter is about discovering your natural strengths and learning how to build on them to shape your career.

Don't worry if you're sitting there thinking, "But I don't know what I'm good at!" That's exactly what we're here to figure out together. The good news? You don't have to know everything right away. You'll discover more about your strengths as you try different things, take on new challenges, and step out of your comfort zone.

Why Skills Matter (And How to Build Them)

Before we dive into the exercises, let's talk about why this is important. In today's world, employers are looking for specific skills for career growth—both technical (like knowing how to use certain software) and soft skills (like communication and teamwork). The more you can build these, the more you'll stand out to potential employers.

But it's not just about getting a job—it's also about figuring out what you enjoy doing. Skills are like puzzle pieces, and as you gather more of them, the clearer the big picture becomes.

Exercise 1: The Skills Inventory

Let's start by making a *Skills Inventory*—a list of things you're already good at and areas where you'd like to improve. Grab a pen or open your notes app and think about these questions:

- **What are your natural strengths?**

  Think about things that come easily to you—are you great at organising, problem-solving, or working with people? Maybe you're a creative thinker or someone who's good at listening and giving advice. Jot down anything that feels like a strength, even if it doesn't seem directly related to a career just yet.

- **What have you learned from past experiences?**

  Have you volunteered, worked part-time, or helped out with family projects? These experiences often help build skills like time management, communication, and teamwork. Don't overlook the small things—every experience counts.

- **Where do you want to grow?**

  Now, think about the skills you *wish* you had or areas where you want to improve. Maybe you'd like to get better at public speaking, learn how to code, or improve your leadership abilities. This is your chance to map out the skills you want to develop over time.

Why Trying Different Jobs Helps

You might be wondering how to figure out what you're good at if you haven't had many jobs yet. That's where trying new things comes in. Don't be afraid to explore part-time work, internships, volunteering, or even taking on freelance gigs. Each experience helps you discover more about what you enjoy and what you don't.

Here's the deal: your first few jobs might not be glamorous, but they're invaluable for learning about yourself and building new skills. Maybe you work in retail and discover you're great at customer service, or maybe you take an internship in marketing and realise you love creative problem-solving. Every job, no matter how small, adds a piece to the puzzle.

Exercise 2: The Job Reflection

Think back to any jobs, internships, or volunteer work you've done. Reflect on the following questions to help you identify what you learned:

- What did you enjoy most about the role?
- What skills did you use in that job, even if they seemed small or simple?
- What did you *not* like about the job? (This helps you figure out what to avoid in the future.)
- Did anyone give you positive feedback on something you did? What was it?

Even if you didn't love the job, you can still pull-out valuable lessons. Maybe working in a fast-food restaurant taught you how to handle pressure, or an office internship helped you get better at managing deadlines. These experiences build the foundation for your future.

The Power of Building Skills Outside of Work

Skills aren't just built in the workplace—they can come from anywhere. Maybe you've picked up photography as a hobby, started your own blog, or organised events for a local club. All of these activities develop useful skills that can transfer into your career.

Let's explore how you can keep growing your skills in all areas of life.

Exercise 3: The Skills Development Plan

Now that you've identified your strengths and areas for growth, it's time to create a *Skills Development Plan*. This doesn't need to be complicated—it's just a roadmap for building the skills you want. Here's how to do it:

- **Pick 3 skills you want to develop.**

    Based on your Skills Inventory, choose three skills you'd like to work on. Maybe it's learning a new software program, improving your communication, or getting better at project management.

- **Set small goals for each skill.**

    Break it down—how can you start developing each skill? It could be taking an online course, practicing with real-world tasks, or asking for feedback from a mentor. Set realistic, achievable goals for each one.

- **Track your progress.**

    Keep a journal or note where you track what you've learned and how you've applied each skill. Over time, you'll see growth—and this will give you concrete examples to use when writing your CV or preparing for interviews.

Why Skills Give You Confidence

The more skills you build, the more confident you'll become—not just in your job search, but in yourself. Knowing what you're good at and being able to show that to potential employers is incredibly empowering. Plus, as you grow, you'll realise that learning new skills doesn't have to be overwhelming. It's all about taking one step at a time.

Chapter 4 Summary

- You have strengths, even if you haven't recognised them yet. Start by creating a Skills Inventory.
- Every job and experience helps you discover more about what you're good at—even the small stuff counts.
- Skills can be built anywhere, not just at work. Hobbies, volunteer work, and even everyday tasks contribute to your growth.
- Use your Skills Development Plan to map out areas for improvement and track your progress over time.

By the end of this chapter, you should have a clearer picture of your strengths and a roadmap for building the skills that matter most to you. Next, we'll dive into how to craft a killer CV that highlights those strengths and gets you noticed by employers.

Chapter 5: Skills That Matter (and How to Get Them)

Now that you've got a clearer idea of what you're good at and where you want to grow, let's talk about the skills that actually *matter* to employers—and how to get them. It's not just about what you know; it's about how well you can apply that knowledge in real-world situations. Some skills are specific to certain industries, while others—known as "soft skills"—are universal.

In this chapter, we're going to explore both. I'll show you the skills that employers value most, how to figure out which ones you need, and the best ways to develop them. Don't worry if you're feeling a little unsure about where to start—that's what this chapter is for.

Why Skills Are the Currency of the Job Market

Employers care about skills because they're the tools that help you get the job done. Your ability to solve problems, work with others, adapt to changing situations, and manage your time are all crucial. And while technical skills are important, soft skills are often what set candidates apart. These are the skills that help you succeed in any environment.

Let's break it down into two categories: hard skills and soft skills.

Hard Skills: The Technical Side of Things

Hard skills are the technical abilities you need to perform specific tasks. Think of these as the "do you know how to use this software or tool?" kind of skills. These vary depending on the job you're aiming for. For example:

- Coding or programming languages (if you're in tech)
- Graphic design software (if you're in creative fields)
- Data analysis (for business or science roles)
- Digital marketing tools (for marketing roles)

Employers want to know that you can hit the ground running with the tools of the trade. But even if you don't have every technical skill listed in a job description, don't panic—many of these can be learned quickly, and employers often value your ability to learn on the job.

Exercise 1: The Job Skills Research

Here's how to figure out which technical skills you'll need for the jobs you're interested in. Grab a pen, your laptop, or your phone, and do the following:

- Find 3 job descriptions for roles that interest you. These could be jobs you want right now or in the future.
- List the hard skills that keep coming up in each job description. For example, if all the jobs mention "Excel proficiency" or "experience with project management software," write those down.
- Highlight the skills you don't have yet. Don't worry about this part—it's normal. This list will help you identify areas to focus on as you build your skills.

Soft Skills: The Game Changers

While hard skills are necessary for specific tasks, soft skills are what make you an effective team member and problem-solver. These are often harder to measure, but they're the ones that make a lasting impression.

Here are some of the top soft skills employers look for:

- **Communication:** Can you clearly express your ideas, listen to others, and adapt your style depending on the situation? Communication is key in every role.
- **Teamwork:** Can you work well with others, collaborate, and contribute to group success?
- **Problem-solving:** Can you identify issues, think critically, and come up with solutions?

- **Adaptability:** Can you stay flexible and positive in changing environments or when things don't go as planned?
- **Time management:** Can you prioritise tasks, meet deadlines, and manage your workload effectively?

These skills may seem basic, but they're invaluable in any job, and they're often what set successful candidates apart.

Exercise 2: Soft Skills Self-Assessment

Let's do a quick assessment of your soft skills. On a scale from 1 to 10 (1 being not confident at all, 10 being very confident), rate yourself on the following:

- Communication
- Teamwork
- Problem-solving
- Adaptability
- Time management

Once you've rated yourself, pick the skill you feel least confident about. We're going to work on improving that one first, so don't worry if you rated yourself low—that's just the starting point.

How to Build the Skills You Need

Now that you've identified the skills you need, let's figure out how to build them. The good news is, you don't need a fancy job or degree to start developing most skills. There are tons of ways to learn and improve, whether you're working, volunteering, or even in your free time.

Exercise 3: The Skills-Building Plan

Here's how to create a plan to build both your hard and soft skills:

- Pick 1 hard skill and 1 soft skill from your previous exercises that you want to focus on.

- Find resources to learn those skills. For hard skills, this might mean online courses (check out platforms like Coursera, Udemy, or LinkedIn Learning) or hands-on practice through a project. For soft skills, it might mean joining a group or club to improve teamwork or taking on a leadership role in a community organisation to boost communication and problem-solving.

- Set small, achievable goals. For example, if you want to improve your communication skills, set a goal to practice active listening in conversations or present your ideas more confidently in group settings. For hard skills, start with beginner-level courses or tutorials and work your way up.

- Track your progress. Keep a journal or note where you track what you've learned and how you've applied it. This will help you see improvement and give you concrete examples for job applications or interviews.

Why Skill-Building is a Lifelong Journey

One thing to remember: building skills is a lifelong process. You're never really done learning. As you grow in your career, you'll continue to refine the skills you have and pick up new ones. The key is to stay curious and adaptable, always looking for ways to improve. It's this mindset that will set you apart from others.

Building skills doesn't have to be overwhelming. Start small, focus on one area at a time, and watch how your confidence grows as you develop new abilities.

Chapter 5 Summary

Let's recap:

- Hard skills are the technical abilities you need for specific jobs. Use job descriptions to identify which ones you should focus on.

- Soft skills like communication, teamwork, and problem-solving are often just as important as technical skills.

- You don't need to master everything at once—create a plan to build the skills you need over time.
- Skill-building is a lifelong process. Stay open to learning, and you'll continue to grow throughout your career.

Next up, we're going to dive into how to present all these wonderful skills in a way that gets you noticed by employers—by crafting a killer CV.

Chapter 6: Why Making Mistakes is Part of the Plan

Here's something they don't tell you enough: mistakes are not just okay—they're essential. If you're trying new things, stepping out of your comfort zone, and growing, you're bound to make mistakes. And that's *good*. Making mistakes means you're learning. No one has ever succeeded without a few stumbles along the way, so let's talk about why mistakes are part of the plan and how you can embrace them as a natural part of your career journey.

The Fear of Failure

Most of us are afraid of making mistakes. We're taught from a young age that failure is something to avoid. But here's the truth: the most successful people in the world didn't get to where they are by avoiding failure. They got there by failing, learning from it, and trying again.

Mistakes are your best teachers. They show you where things went wrong, what you need to work on, and how you can do better next time. The key is to change your mindset—don't look at mistakes as failures; look at them as learnings from career failures and opportunities to grow.

Exercise 1: Reframing a Past Mistake

Let's start by thinking back to a mistake you've made in the past—something that didn't go the way you wanted, whether it was a job application that didn't pan out, a project that didn't work, or even a personal decision. Write down the following:

- **What happened?** Describe the situation.
- **How did you feel at the time?** Be honest. Did it feel like a failure? Were you embarrassed or frustrated?
- **What did you learn?** Looking back now, what did that experience teach you? How did it help you grow or change your approach?

Now, take a moment to reflect. Often, we don't see the value in our mistakes until later. But with time, they become lessons. This exercise helps you start viewing mistakes as part of your learning process rather than something to avoid.

How to Learn from Mistakes

The real power of making mistakes lies in how you respond to them. Instead of beating yourself up when things don't go perfectly, use the experience to improve. Here's a simple three-step process for learning from workplace mistakes:

- **Acknowledge it**. It's important to admit when something didn't work out. Don't shy away from it or ignore it—face it head-on.
- **Reflect on it**. Ask yourself: Why didn't this work? What could I have done differently? Were there factors beyond my control, or was there something I missed?
- **Make a plan to do better next time.** What will you change in the future? How can you apply what you've learned from this mistake to improve?

Every mistake gives you the opportunity to adjust and refine your approach. The people who succeed aren't the ones who never make mistakes—they're the ones who learn and improve from them.

Exercise 2: The Growth Mindset Shift

In psychology, there's something called a *growth mindset*—the belief that abilities and intelligence can be developed through dedication and hard work. People with a growth mindset view mistakes as part of the process. In contrast, a *fixed mindset* believes that abilities are set in stone, and mistakes are a sign of failure.

Let's practice shifting to a growth mindset. Think about something you're struggling with—maybe it's a skill you're working on or a job application that didn't go as planned. Ask yourself these questions:

- **What can I learn from this experience?** Focus on the lessons, not the disappointment.
- **What can I do differently next time?** Instead of feeling stuck, think about how you can improve.
- **How have I grown already?** Reflect on the progress you've made, even if you're not where you want to be yet.

This mindset shift is key to embracing mistakes and seeing them as part of your growth. It takes practice, but over time, you'll start to view challenges and setbacks as opportunities to improve.

Why Mistakes Build Resilience

Here's another benefit of making mistakes: they help you build resilience. The more you learn to handle setbacks and keep moving forward, the stronger you become. Resilience is the ability to bounce back from challenges, and it's one of the most valuable qualities you can develop in your career (and life).

Resilience isn't about avoiding mistakes—it's about learning how to get up, dust yourself off, and keep going when things don't go your way. It's about believing in your ability to overcome difficulties and trusting that every setback is just a stepping stone to success.

Exercise 3: Building Resilience Through Reflection

Let's practice resilience by reflecting on how you've overcome challenges in the past. Think of a time when something didn't go as planned, but you managed to move forward anyway. Write down your answers to these questions:

- What challenge did you face?
- How did you handle it?
- What strengths did you use to overcome the situation?
- How did you feel after you made it through?

By reflecting on past challenges, you remind yourself that you've already overcome difficulties before—and you can do it again. Each time you face a setback and push through it, you're building your resilience muscle.

Why Perfection Isn't the Goal

A lot of people hold themselves back by striving for perfection. They want to get everything right the first time, and if they can't, they're afraid to even try. But here's the thing—perfection doesn't exist. There's no such thing as a perfect career, a perfect job application, or a perfect path.

The goal isn't perfection—the goal is progress. As long as you're learning, growing, and taking steps forward, you're on the right track. Don't let the fear of making mistakes stop you from trying new things. The more you take action, the more you'll learn, and the closer you'll get to your goals.

Chapter 6 Summary

Here's what we've covered:

- Mistakes are part of the learning process. Embrace them and learn from them.
- Shifting to a growth mindset helps you see mistakes as opportunities for growth, not signs of failure.
- Mistakes build resilience—the ability to bounce back from challenges is key to long-term success.
- Perfection isn't the goal—progress is.

So, the next time something doesn't go as planned, remember, you're learning. Every mistake is teaching you something valuable, and with each lesson, you're getting closer to where you want to be.

In the next chapter, we'll talk about how to build your confidence, even when you're feeling unsure or facing setbacks. Confidence isn't about having all the answers—it's about trusting yourself to figure things out as you go.

Chapter 7: Building Confidence Without Faking It

Let's talk about confidence. You've probably heard people say things like, "Fake it till you make it," but here's the thing—confidence isn't about pretending you know everything or acting like you have it all together. True confidence comes from trusting yourself to handle whatever comes your way, even when you don't have all the answers.

In this chapter, we'll explore how to build real confidence, not by faking it, but by focusing on preparation, practice, and trusting your ability to figure things out. You don't need to have everything sorted to be confident—you just need to believe in your capacity to learn and grow. Ready? Let's dive in.

Why Confidence Matters

Confidence isn't just about feeling good—it's a tool that helps you navigate challenges, take risks, and seize opportunities. Employers value confident candidates because they trust that these individuals can handle responsibility, solve problems, and contribute to a team. But it's not just about impressing others—confidence helps you take action, even when you're unsure of the outcome.

Here's the secret: confidence is built through action. The more you do something, the more comfortable you become with it. And even if you stumble, you'll know that you have the resilience to keep going.

Exercise 1: Your Confidence Baseline

Let's start by figuring out where you're currently at with your confidence. Take a moment to reflect on the following questions:

- In which areas of life or work do you feel most confident? Why?
- In which areas do you feel the least confident? What causes that feeling?
- What situations make you feel unsure of yourself?

Write down your answers. This exercise is about recognising where your confidence is strong and where it might need a little work. It's okay if you feel unsure in some areas—that's normal. We'll work on building that up.

Why Preparation Builds Confidence

One of the best ways to boost your confidence is through preparation. Think about it: if you've prepared for something—whether it's an interview, a presentation, or even a new job—you naturally feel more at ease because you know what to expect. Preparation doesn't mean overthinking or obsessing over every detail—it means taking the time to understand the situation and plan your approach.

For example, if you're nervous about a job interview, preparing by researching the company, practicing common questions, and thinking about how to showcase your skills will make you feel more confident when the day comes.

Exercise 2: The Confidence Boost Through Preparation

Let's practice building confidence through preparation. Think about an upcoming challenge—maybe it's an interview, a big project, or even a networking event. Then follow these steps:

- **Research:** Learn everything you can about the situation. If it's an interview, research the company and the role. If it's a presentation, understand your audience.
- **Plan:** Write down a few key points you want to highlight or focus on. For interviews, this might be your strengths and experiences. For a project, it could be your main ideas and the steps you'll take to achieve them.
- **Practice:** Go over your plan, rehearse your points, and visualise yourself succeeding. The more familiar you are with the situation, the less intimidating it becomes.

By preparing in advance, you give yourself the mental tools to handle whatever comes your way. This preparation turns uncertainty into confidence.

Confidence Without Perfection

A common mistake is believing that you need to be perfect to be confident. Perfectionism can actually undermine your confidence because it sets an impossible standard. The truth is, confidence isn't about always getting things right—it's about trusting yourself to handle things, even when they don't go perfectly.

Everyone makes mistakes. The key to confidence is knowing that you can recover from them. You don't have to be perfect to be successful—you just have to be willing to learn and adapt.

Exercise 3: The "Good Enough" Approach

To help let go of perfectionism, try adopting a "good enough" mindset. The next time you're working on something, ask yourself:

- Does this meet the main goals or requirements?
- Am I satisfied with the quality, even if it's not perfect?

If the answer is yes, then stop trying to push for perfection. Delivering something "good enough" is often more than sufficient, and it will help you build confidence by focusing on progress, not perfection.

How to Handle Imposter Syndrome

At some point, nearly everyone feels like they don't belong or aren't qualified enough for a job or task. This is called *imposter syndrome*, and it's that nagging voice in your head telling you, "You don't really know what you're doing," even when you're perfectly capable.

Here's the thing: imposter syndrome thrives in silence. The more you acknowledge it, the less power it has. Recognise when those feelings come up and remind yourself that you've earned your place through hard work and learning. Confidence isn't about knowing everything—it's about trusting that you can figure things out as you go.

Exercise 4: Rewriting Your Story

When imposter syndrome strikes, it's easy to focus on all the reasons why you think you're not good enough. Let's flip the script. Think of a recent time when you felt like an imposter. Now, write down the following:

- **What were the negative thoughts you had?** For example, "I don't deserve to be here," or "Everyone else is smarter than me."
- **What's the truth?** What evidence do you have that proves those thoughts wrong? For example, "I got this job because I have the skills," or "I've worked hard to get where I am."

By rewriting your internal dialogue, you remind yourself that you've earned your place, and it's okay to feel unsure sometimes. The important thing is to keep moving forward, despite the doubts.

Confidence Comes From Action

The final piece of the confidence puzzle is taking action. Confidence doesn't come from thinking about doing something—it comes from actually doing it. The more you take action, the more your confidence grows.

Here's a simple truth: confidence is built step by step, one small win at a time. Whether it's tackling a new project, speaking up in a meeting, or reaching out to someone for advice, each action you take builds your confidence for the next step.

Chapter 7 Summary

Let's recap:

- Confidence isn't about faking it or being perfect—it's about trusting yourself to handle things, even when you don't have all the answers.
- Preparation is one of the best ways to build confidence. The more you prepare, the more familiar and comfortable you'll feel.
- Perfection isn't the goal—progress is. Don't let the desire for perfection hold you back from taking action.
- Imposter syndrome is common, but it doesn't define you. Rewriting your internal story helps combat those feelings of doubt.
- Confidence comes from action. Every small step you take builds the foundation for stronger confidence in the future.

Next, we'll dive into the nuts and bolts of landing a job, from writing a CV that stands out to acing interviews. But remember, confidence is your secret weapon—trust yourself, and you'll be surprised at how far you can go.

Part 2 Summary: Practical Steps to Building Your Career

By now, you've built a solid foundation for taking those next steps in your career journey. Part 2 has been all about getting practical, taking what you've learned about yourself and turning it into action. You've explored the key skills you need, how to develop them, and how to present them to employers in a way that gets you noticed.

Here's a quick recap of what we've covered:

- **Figuring Out What You're Good At**

    In Chapter 4, we worked on identifying your strengths and where you want to grow. You learned how every job and experience adds something valuable, even if it doesn't seem obvious at the time. Building skills is a lifelong journey, and it starts with recognising your own unique talents.

- **Skills That Matter (And How to Get Them)**

    Chapter 5 was all about figuring out which skills employers are looking for and how you can start building them. From technical (hard) skills to the ever-important soft skills like communication and teamwork, you now know how to create a plan for developing these, no matter where you're starting from.

- **Why Making Mistakes is Part of the Plan**

    Mistakes are not failures—they're opportunities to learn and grow. In Chapter 6, we talked about how to shift your mindset, embrace mistakes as part of the process, and use them to build resilience. Learning from setbacks is what helps you move forward stronger and smarter.

- **Building Confidence Without Faking It**

    Chapter 7 showed you that confidence isn't about pretending to know everything—it's about trusting yourself to figure things out as you go. Through preparation, letting go of perfectionism, and taking action, you've learned how to build real confidence, one step at a time.

Looking Ahead: What's Next?

Now that you've laid the groundwork, you're ready to put everything into action. Part 3 is going to focus on how to land that job—how to craft a CV that truly reflects your strengths, how to prepare for interviews, and how to network in a way that feels natural (not awkward!).

You've already got what it takes to succeed. It's just a matter of showing the world what you're capable of. So take a deep breath, trust yourself, and get ready to make things happen.

Part 3 Introduction: Landing the Job (Without Losing Your Mind)

Alright, here we are—this is where all your self-reflection, skill-building, and confidence work come together. In Part 3, we're going to focus on turning everything you've learned into real, actionable steps to help you land a job. From writing a CV that stands out to preparing for interviews and building your network, we're covering everything you need to start your job search with confidence.

The job search process can feel overwhelming at times but remember—you don't have to tackle it all at once. You've already built a strong foundation in Parts 1 and 2. Now, it's about showing the world what you're capable of and getting the practical side of things in place. We're going to break it down into manageable steps, making the process feel more like a journey of discovery than a stressful sprint to the finish line.

You've got the tools, the skills, and the confidence—now it's time to land that job!

Chapter 8: How to Write a CV That Gets Noticed

Your CV (or résumé, depending on where you are) is often the first thing employers see, and first impressions matter. But here's the trick: your CV isn't just a list of your past jobs and education. It's a marketing tool. It's a way to show potential employers why *you* are the best fit for the role they're offering. So, let's dive into how you can craft a CV that stands out from the stack and gets you noticed.

What Your CV Really Says About You

Think of your CV as your personal highlight reel. It's not just about what you've done, but how you present what you've done. Your goal is to clearly show how your skills, experiences, and achievements match the job you're applying for. It's less about *what* you've done and more about *how* what you've done makes you a great fit for the role.

Let's start by breaking down the key components of a CV and how you can make each section work for you.

The Key Components of a Great CV

- **Personal Statement / Profile**

  This is a short paragraph at the top of your CV that introduces you to potential employers. Think of it as your elevator pitch—who you are, what you offer, and why you're a great fit for the job. Keep it concise and focused, highlighting career achievements and your most relevant skills and career goals.

- **Work Experience**

  List your work experience in reverse chronological order, starting with your most recent job. For each position, focus on achievements rather than just listing duties. Employers want to see the impact you made, so use bullet points to highlight accomplishments like "increased sales by 20%" or "led a team of 5 on a successful project." Tailor this section to the job you're applying for, emphasising the skills and experiences that match the role.

- **Education**

    Include your educational background but focus on what's relevant. If you have work experience, this section can be shorter. If you're just starting out, you can highlight key projects, coursework, or extracurricular activities that demonstrate your skills.

- **Skills**

    This section is where you can showcase both your hard and soft skills. Include any technical abilities (like software proficiency) and soft skills (like communication and teamwork). Make sure to align your skills with the job description, showing how you meet their specific needs.

- **Other Sections (Optional)**

    Depending on the job, you might want to include sections like "Certifications," "Volunteer Experience," or "Awards." These can help paint a fuller picture of who you are and what you bring to the table.

Exercise 1: Crafting Your Personal Statement

Let's start with your personal statement. This is often the trickiest part because you need to sum yourself up in just a few sentences. Here's a template to help you get started:

- **Who are you?**

    Begin by stating your current role or your professional identity. For example: "I am a recent graduate with a passion for marketing" or "I am an experienced project manager with a track record of delivering successful campaigns."

- **What do you offer?**

    Highlight the key skills and experiences that make you stand out. For example: "With experience in social media management and content creation, I bring a creative approach to brand building."

- **Why should they hire you?**

    End by explaining why you're a great fit for the role you're applying for. For example: "I am eager to contribute my skills in digital marketing to help drive engagement and growth for your company."

Now, take a few minutes to draft your personal statement. Keep it focused and remember to tailor it to the specific role you're applying for.

How to Tailor Your CV for Each Job

One of the biggest mistakes people make is sending out the same CV for every job. Employers can tell when a CV hasn't been customised, and it doesn't leave a good impression. Instead, take the time to tailor your CV for each role you apply for. It shows that you're genuinely interested in the position and that you've taken the time to understand what the employer is looking for.

Here's how to tailor your CV:

- Use the job description as a guide. Highlight the skills and experiences they're asking for, and make sure those are front and centre on your CV.
- Reword your personal statement. Align it with the company's values and the role's responsibilities.
- Adjust your bullet points. Emphasise the parts of your experience that are most relevant to the job.

Exercise 2: Tailoring Your CV

Pick a job posting that interests you and compare it to your current CV. Ask yourself:

- What keywords from the job posting can I include in my CV?
- How can I rephrase my experience to better match the job description?
- Are there any skills or experiences I should add or remove to make my CV more relevant?

Spend some time editing your CV to better align it with the specific job. This step can make a huge difference in getting noticed.

Design and Layout: Keep It Simple

Your CV should be easy to read. Fancy fonts and graphics might look cool, but they can distract from the content. Stick to clean, simple formatting:

- Use a professional font like Arial or Calibri and keep the font size between 10 and 12 points.
- Use bullet points to break up text and make it easier to scan.
- Stick to reverse chronological order for work experience.
- Keep it to one or two pages—employers don't have time to sift through a novel.

Exercise 3: The Final CV Checklist

Before you send off your CV, go through this quick checklist:

- Does your personal statement clearly highlight who you are and what you offer?
- Is your CV tailored to the job you're applying for?
- Have you used bullet points to make your accomplishments stand out?
- Is the layout clean and easy to read?
- Have you double-checked for typos and grammatical errors?

Why Your CV is Only the Beginning

Remember, your CV is just the start of the process. It's the foot in the door, the thing that gets you noticed. But once you've crafted a CV that shows off your skills and experiences, it's time to get ready for the next steps—cover letters, interviews, and networking. Each piece builds on the last, and together, they create a powerful case for why you're the right person for the job.

Chapter 8 Summary

Here's what we covered:

- Your CV is a marketing tool, not just a list of jobs. Focus on highlighting your accomplishments and skills.
- A great CV includes a strong personal statement, tailored work experience, and relevant skills.
- Always tailor your CV to each job, using the job description as a guide.
- Keep your layout simple and professional—it's about clarity, not flash.

Next, we'll dive into how to prepare for interviews—because landing the interview is just the first step. Let's get you ready to impress!

Chapter 9: Acing the Interview

You've made it past the first hurdle—your CV caught their attention, and now you've landed an interview. Congratulations! But now comes the next step: showing up as your best, most confident self during the interview. This is your chance to prove that everything on your CV isn't just talk—you've got the skills, the attitude, and the potential to be exactly what they need.

In this chapter, we'll break down how to prepare for interviews so you can walk in (or log in, if it's virtual!) with confidence. You'll learn what to expect, how to handle common behavioural questions, and how to let your personality shine without nerves taking over.

Why Preparation is Key

Just like with your CV, preparation is your secret weapon. The more you know about the company, the role, and even yourself, the more comfortable and confident you'll feel. Interviews aren't just about answering questions—they're about having a conversation. You're not just proving that you're a good fit for the company; you're also figuring out if the company is a good fit for *you*.

Exercise 1: Research, Research, Research

Before any interview, you need to do some homework. Research the company, the role, and the industry so you can speak confidently about why you want the job and how you fit in. Here's a checklist to guide your research:

- **The Company:**

    What does the company do? What's their mission? What kind of work environment do they promote? Have they been in the news recently for any major projects or successes?

- **The Role:**

    What are the key responsibilities? What skills are they looking for? What challenges might you face in this role, and how can you contribute to overcoming them?

- **The Industry:**

    Are there any major trends, changes, or challenges in the industry? How do you think these will impact the company?

Write down your key findings in bullet points. This will not only help you feel prepared but will also show the interviewer that you've done your homework, which makes a great first impression.

Common Interview Questions and How to Answer Them

Interviews can feel intimidating, especially when you're hit with questions you didn't see coming. But don't worry—most interviews include a set of common job interview questions, and with a bit of preparation, you can answer them confidently.

Here are some common interview questions and how to tackle them:

- **"Tell me about yourself."**

    This is your opportunity to give a brief, engaging overview of your background. Focus on your professional journey—what brought you to this point, and how your experiences and skills make you a good fit for the role. Keep it relevant to the job you're applying for and avoid rambling about personal details.

- **"Why do you want this job?"**

    Here's where your research comes in. Explain why the role excites you, how it aligns with your career goals, and why you think the company is a great fit. Mention something specific about the company that attracted you—this shows you've done your homework.

- **"What are your strengths?"**

    Choose 2-3 strengths that are relevant to the job and give examples of how you've used those strengths in previous roles or projects. Don't just list adjectives—use real-life examples to back them up.

- **"What's your biggest weakness?"**

    The classic trick question! The goal here is to be honest but also to show self-awareness and a willingness to improve. Choose a real weakness but explain how you're working to overcome it. For example: "I used to struggle with time management, but I've started using tools like Trello to organise my workload, and I've seen a big improvement."

- **"Tell me about a time you faced a challenge at work and how you handled it."**

    Use the STAR method:
    - Situation: Briefly describe the situation.
    - Task: Explain what the task was.
    - Action: Detail the specific actions you took.
    - Result: Share the positive outcome or lesson learned.

By preparing answers for these common questions, you'll feel more at ease during the interview. The goal is to be prepared, but not rehearsed—you want to sound natural and authentic.

Exercise 2: Practice Makes Perfect

The best way to feel confident in an interview is to practice. Find a friend, family member, or mentor and ask them to conduct a mock interview with you. Use the common questions from the list above, and practice answering them aloud. Pay attention to your body language, eye contact, and tone of voice.

Here's a simple structure for your mock interview:

- **Start with a handshake (or greeting, for virtual interviews).**

    Make sure you come across as approachable and friendly right from the start.

- **Answer the common questions.**

    Focus on giving clear, concise, and engaging answers. Use real-life examples whenever possible.

- **Ask for feedback.**

    After the mock interview, ask for feedback. Were your answers clear? Did you come across as confident? Did you make good eye contact and maintain a positive tone?

This exercise will help you get comfortable with the interview process so that when the real thing comes, you'll feel prepared and in control.

Virtual Interviews: What's Different?

With more and more interviews happening online, it's important to understand the unique challenges of virtual interviews. While the questions might be the same, the setting is different, and you need to make sure you're prepared for the tech side of things.

Here's how to ace a virtual interview:

- **Check your tech.**

    Make sure your internet connection is strong, your webcam and microphone are working, and your interview platform (Zoom, Teams, etc.) is set up correctly.

- **Find the right space.**

    Choose a quiet, well-lit area where you won't be interrupted. Make sure your background is clean and professional—avoid clutter or distractions.

- **Look at the camera, not the screen.**

    This helps you maintain virtual eye contact, which makes a big difference in how engaged you appear.

- **Stay engaged.**

    Without the natural body language and presence of an in-person interview, it's easy for virtual interviews to feel distant. Make an extra effort to smile, nod, and stay animated to show you're engaged and interested.

Asking Questions: The Interview Goes Both Ways

Remember, an interview isn't just about them evaluating you—it's also your chance to evaluate *them*. Asking thoughtful questions not only shows that you're interested, but it also helps you figure out if this company and role are the right fit for you.

Here are some good questions to ask:

- **"What does success look like in this role?"**

    This helps you understand the company's expectations and how you'll be measured.

- **"Can you tell me more about the team I'll be working with?"**

    This gives you insight into the company culture and how you'll fit into the team dynamic.

- **"What are the biggest challenges the company is currently facing?"**

    This shows you're thinking big-picture and want to understand the company's priorities.

- **"What opportunities are there for growth and development?"**

    This signals that you're thinking long-term and are interested in advancing within the company.

Exercise 3: Prepare Your Questions

Before your next interview, write down 3-5 questions you'd like to ask the interviewer. Make sure they're relevant to the company, the role, and your career goals. Asking good questions shows that you're engaged and serious about the position.

Chapter 9 Summary

Let's recap:

- Preparation is the key to feeling confident in interviews. Do your research on the company, the role, and the industry.
- Practice answering common interview questions so you're ready when they come up.
- For virtual interviews, make sure your tech is working, and stay engaged by looking at the camera and using positive body language.
- Interviews are a two-way street—ask thoughtful questions to show your interest and evaluate if the company is the right fit for you.

Now that you've mastered the art of the interview, we'll dive into the next chapter—how to network without feeling awkward and build connections that can help you land your dream job.

Chapter 10: Networking Without Feeling Awkward

Let's be honest, networking can feel awkward. For a lot of people, the idea of walking into a room full of strangers or reaching out to someone online feels intimidating. But here's the thing: networking isn't about forcing fake conversations or pretending to be someone you're not. It's about building *genuine* connections with people who can help you, and whom you can help, too.

In this chapter, we'll break down effective networking strategies in a way that feels natural and comfortable for you. Whether you're connecting in person or online, I'll show you how to build professional connections that could lead to exciting career opportunities down the road.

Why Networking Matters

You've probably heard the phrase, "It's not what you know, it's who you know." While it's not the *whole* story, there's a lot of truth to it. Many jobs aren't even advertised; they're filled through personal connections and referrals. That's why networking is so important—it opens doors that you didn't even know existed.

But networking isn't just about landing jobs. It's about learning from others, getting advice, and building a support system of people who can help you grow in your career.

Exercise 1: Map Your Current Network

Before you start building new connections, it's helpful to think about the network you already have. Grab a pen and paper and write down the people you already know who could help with your career. These could include:

- Former colleagues
- Friends or family members

- Professors or mentors
- People from internships, volunteer work, or part-time jobs

Your network is probably bigger than you think! Even if the people you know don't work in your field, they might know someone who does. List their names, and then consider reaching out to let them know what kind of opportunities you're looking for.

How to Network (Without Feeling Awkward)

Now that you've identified your current network, let's talk about how to build new connections in a way that feels natural. Networking doesn't have to be stiff or transactional. It's all about finding ways to connect authentically.

Here are a few approaches that work:

- **Start Small**

  Networking doesn't always mean attending huge events. Start by reaching out to someone in your existing network—maybe a former colleague or classmate. Ask for advice or a quick chat over coffee. This helps you ease into networking without feeling overwhelmed.

- **Leverage Social Media**

  Platforms like LinkedIn are great for professional networking. Follow people in your field, engage with their content by liking or commenting, and send personalised connection requests. When you reach out, mention something specific about their work that you admire—it shows you're genuinely interested in them, not just looking to gain something.

- **Be Curious**

  Networking is about learning, not just asking for favours. Ask people about their career paths, their experiences, and their challenges. Most people enjoy sharing their stories and giving advice, especially when you approach them with genuine curiosity.

- **Offer Help**

    Networking is a two-way street. Don't just think about what others can do for you—consider what you can offer them. Whether it's sharing an interesting article, introducing them to someone in your network, or offering to help with a project, giving back strengthens relationships.

Exercise 2: The LinkedIn Connection Plan

If you're feeling unsure about how to connect with people online, start with LinkedIn. It's a professional space, which makes it a bit easier to reach out without it feeling awkward. Here's a simple plan to get started:

- **Update Your Profile**

    Make sure your LinkedIn profile reflects your skills, experiences, and career goals. Your profile is your digital business card, so make it shine.

- **Find 3 People to Connect With**

    Look for professionals in your field, industry leaders, or even people who work at companies you're interested in. Send them a connection request but personalise your message. For example: "Hi [Name], I saw your recent post about [topic], and it really resonated with me. I'm currently working in [industry/role] and would love to connect and learn more about your experience."

- **Engage with Content**

    Don't just connect—interact! Comment on posts, share interesting articles, and contribute to discussions. This keeps you visible and shows that you're engaged in your industry.

In-Person Networking: Making It Less Awkward

In-person networking events can feel a little daunting, especially if you're not naturally outgoing. But with the right mindset, they don't have to be. Here's how to overcome networking anxiety make in-person networking a little less awkward:

- **Set a Goal**

    Don't feel like you have to talk to everyone in the room. Set a simple goal—like having 3 meaningful conversations—and focus on quality over quantity.

- **Start with Small Talk**

    Small talk can be the gateway to more meaningful conversations. Ask about the event, the person's work, or even comment on something light like the venue or food. Small talk helps break the ice and leads into more substantive topics.

- **Follow Up**

    After the event, follow up with the people you met. Send them a quick email or LinkedIn message, thanking them for the conversation and expressing interest in staying in touch. This keeps the connection alive and shows you're serious about building relationships.

Exercise 3: Prepare for an In-Person Event

If you have a networking event coming up, it's a good idea to prepare. Here's a quick checklist:

- **Research the event.**

    What kind of event is it? Who will be attending? Having an idea of the event's focus will help you feel more prepared.

- **Prepare your introduction.**

    When someone asks, "So, what do you do?" you don't want to be caught off guard. Prepare a short, natural-sounding introduction about yourself. For example "Hi, I'm [Your Name], and I work in [your field]. I'm really interested in [specific topic], and I'm here to learn more about how people are tackling [related challenge]."

- **Have a few conversation starters ready.**

  Think of a few questions you can ask to keep conversations flowing. For example: "What brought you to this event?" or "What's something exciting happening in your industry right now?"

Chapter 10 Summary

Let's recap:

- Networking is about building *genuine* connections, not forcing awkward conversations.
- Start with your existing network—there are likely people who can help you already.
- Whether you're networking online or in person, focus on being curious, offering help, and building authentic relationships.
- Follow up with people after events or online interactions to keep the connection going.

With these tips and exercises, networking won't feel as daunting. Remember, it's a skill like any other—the more you practice, the easier and more natural it becomes. Next, we'll wrap up Part 3 and get ready to dive into the final steps for landing that dream job.

Part 3 Summary: Landing the Job

Congratulations—you've made it through the most practical part of the book, where we've turned self-reflection and skill-building into concrete steps for landing a job. Let's quickly recap what we've covered:

- **Writing a CV That Gets Noticed**

    In Chapter 8, you learned how to craft a CV that highlights your skills and accomplishments, making you stand out to employers. We covered the importance of tailoring your CV for each job, using the job description as your guide, and keeping your layout clean and professional.

- **Acing the Interview**

    Chapter 9 was all about preparing for interviews, both in-person and virtual. From answering common questions to using the STAR method for behavioural questions, you now have the tools to walk into an interview with confidence. We also covered how to ask thoughtful questions that show your interest in the company.

- **Networking Without Feeling Awkward**

    Chapter 10 tackled the art of networking, both online and in person. You learned how to build genuine connections, engage on platforms like LinkedIn, and navigate networking events without feeling overwhelmed.

What's Next?

Now that you've got the tools to create a winning CV, ace interviews, and build your professional network, you're ready to take the final steps toward landing the job of your dreams. In the next section, we'll focus on how to navigate the early stages of your career and thrive in your first job.

Remember, each of these steps builds on the last. Stay patient, keep practicing, and don't be afraid to take risks. You've got this!

Part 4 Introduction: Thriving in the Workplace (And Beyond)

Congratulations! You've made it through the job search process—you've written your CV, aced the interview, and even built up a network of connections. Now comes the next big step: thriving in the workplace.

But this part isn't just about surviving your first job—it's about finding your rhythm, setting yourself up for success, and continuing to grow both personally and professionally. Your career doesn't stop when you land your first job. In fact, it's only just beginning.

In Part 4, we're going to explore how to make the most of your first job, how to master workplace social skills, how to navigate workplace dynamics, and how to keep growing in your career without burning out. We'll also talk about the importance of maintaining balance between work and life, and how to ensure you're not just thriving in the workplace but in *all* aspects of your life.

So, let's dive into this new chapter of your journey—here's to building a career (and life) that you truly enjoy.

Chapter 11: Starting Your First Job (And Doing It Well)

Landing your first job is an exciting milestone, but it can also feel a bit overwhelming. You've made it through the job search process, but now you're stepping into a new environment, with new expectations and responsibilities. The first few weeks and months in a job are crucial—they set the tone for how you'll be seen in the company and how quickly you'll get comfortable in your role.In this chapter, we'll talk about how to make the best first impression, how to navigate your new workplace with confidence, and what you can do to ensure that you're set up for success in your first job. Don't worry—you don't have to know everything right away. We're going to break it down step by step.

Why the First Few Weeks Matter

The first few weeks in any new job are all about learning the ropes and navigating office culture while building relationships. Your goal in this early stage is to absorb as much information as possible while also showing that you're capable, reliable, and eager to contribute. It's not about being perfect—it's about being present and engaged.

During this time, people will form their first impressions of you, and those impressions can stick. But don't stress—it's not about impressing everyone with how much you know. It's about showing that you're willing to learn, ask questions, and get involved.

Exercise 1: Setting Yourself Up for Success

Before you start your new job, take a moment to set some personal goals for your first month. Think about what you want to accomplish, both in terms of your own learning and how you want to be perceived by your colleagues. Here are some prompts to help you set your goals:

- **What do you want to learn?**

    Is there a specific skill or process you need to master in your role? Make a list of things you want to get a handle on in your first month.

- **How do you want to be perceived?**

    Think about the qualities you want to be known for. Do you want to be seen as dependable, proactive, a team player? Write down 2-3 traits you want to focus on.

- **What relationships do you want to build?**

    Your success in any job depends on the relationships you build with your colleagues. Make it a goal to introduce yourself to key people in your department and beyond.

By setting these goals, you'll have a clear focus for your first few weeks. This helps you stay proactive and gives you direction as you settle in.

How to Make a Great First Impression

Making a good first impression at work isn't about being the loudest or trying to show off. It's about being present, showing respect, and demonstrating that you're ready to contribute. Here are a few simple ways to make sure your first impression is a positive one:

- **Introduce Yourself Confidently**

    When you first start, introduce yourself to as many colleagues as you can. A simple, "Hi, I'm [Your Name], I'm new here and excited to join the team!" goes a long way. Don't be shy, people expect new hires to introduce themselves. Make eye contact, smile, and give a firm handshake (if in person).

- **Dress for Success**

    Your appearance is often the first thing people notice, so dress appropriately for the workplace. If you're not sure what's expected, look at what your colleagues are wearing or ask about the dress code. It's always better to be slightly overdressed at first until you gauge the company's style.

- **Observe Company Culture**

    Each workplace has its own office culture, and it's important to take note of how things are done. Are meetings formal or relaxed? Do people communicate mostly via email or face-to-face? Spend your first week observing how people interact and adjust your behaviour accordingly.

- **Be Punctual**

    This might seem obvious, but being on time—whether it's for meetings, starting your workday, or delivering tasks—shows that you respect other people's time and take your responsibilities seriously.

- **Ask Questions**

    Don't be afraid to ask for clarification when you're unsure about something. It's better to ask questions early on than to make assumptions and get things wrong. People will appreciate your willingness to learn.

- **Take Notes**

    During your first few weeks, you'll be given a lot of information. Keep a notebook handy and write down important points, tasks, and processes. This shows that you're organised and that you value what's being taught to you.

- **Show Enthusiasm**

    No one expects you to know everything, but showing enthusiasm and a positive attitude goes a long way. Be open to new challenges, and don't be afraid to volunteer for tasks or projects.

Exercise 1: First Impressions Role-Play

Pair up with a friend or colleague. Practice introducing yourself confidently and exchanging small talk. Provide feedback on body language and tone.

Navigating Workplace Culture

Every workplace has its own culture—its unwritten rules about how things are done. Some workplaces are laid back and casual, while others are more formal and structured. Understanding and adapting to your workplace culture is key to fitting in and succeeding.

Here's how you can get a sense of your workplace culture:

- **Observe How Others Behave**

    Pay attention to how your colleagues interact with each other, how they communicate with management, and how they handle work tasks. This will give you a sense of the workplace norms.

- **Ask About Expectations**

    If you're unsure about something—whether it's how to dress for work, how formal meetings should be, or how deadlines are handled—don't hesitate to ask. Your manager or team members will appreciate your desire to understand the culture.

- **Adapt Without Losing Yourself**

    While it's important to fit in, don't feel like you have to change who you are to succeed. Be yourself but be mindful of the dynamics around you. Striking this balance will help you navigate the culture while staying authentic.

Exercise 2: Workplace Observation

During your first week on the job, take some time each day to observe the workplace culture. Use these prompts to guide your observations:

- **Communication Style:** Are people more formal or casual when they communicate? How do they address each other?
- **Work Pace:** Is the office fast paced, with quick turnarounds, or does the team take a more measured approach to tasks?
- **Team Interaction:** How do colleagues interact—do they collaborate often, or is most work done independently?

By actively observing, you'll quickly get a feel for how things work in your new environment, making it easier to fit in and contribute.

The Importance of Asking for Feedback

One of the most valuable things you can do early in your career is ask for feedback. This shows that you're serious about improving and that you're open to learning. It also gives you insights into how others see your work and where you can grow.

- **Schedule a Check-In:** After your first month, ask your manager for a quick check-in to review how things are going. Use this time to ask for feedback on your performance and areas where you can improve.
- **Be Open to Constructive Criticism:** No one is perfect, especially when they're just starting out. Don't take feedback personally—see it as a tool to help you get better.
- **Act on Feedback:** Once you receive feedback, make an effort to improve in the areas mentioned. This shows that you're committed to growing in your role.

Chapter 11 Summary

Here's what we covered:

- The first few weeks in a new job are crucial for setting the tone—focus on learning, building relationships, and making a positive first impression.
- Set personal goals for your first month on the job to stay focused and proactive.
- Navigating workplace culture is about observing how things work and adapting without losing your sense of self.
- Asking for feedback early on helps you grow and shows that you're committed to improving in your role.

Starting your first job can be exciting, but it can also be a bit nerve-wracking. Remember, you don't have to know everything right away. It's all about being open to learning and showing that you're ready to contribute. In the next chapter, we'll talk about how to keep growing in your career and how to take on more responsibilities as you gain confidence.

Chapter 12: Mastering Workplace Social Skills and Etiquette

You've landed your first job—congratulations! But getting hired is just the start. Now you're stepping into a new environment filled with people, expectations, and rules (some of which aren't written down). For many young professionals, one of the biggest challenges isn't the work itself but figuring out how to fit in, navigate social dynamics, and make the right impression.

This chapter is all about helping you master the unspoken aspects of workplace life: how to present yourself, communicate effectively, and build relationships without feeling out of place. Let's dive into the key social skills and etiquette tips you'll need to thrive.

Workplace Etiquette 101

Workplace etiquette is more than just saying "please" and "thank you." It's about being respectful, considerate, and professional in all your interactions. Here's how to ensure your etiquette is on point:

- **Email Etiquette**

    Emails are one of the most common forms of workplace communication. Keep your emails professional—use proper greetings, be concise, and proofread before hitting send. Avoid slang or emojis unless you're sure it's part of the culture. For example:

    - **Good**: "Hi [Colleague's Name], I wanted to follow up on [topic]. Please let me know if you need any additional information."

    - **Not so good**: "Hey! Just checking in—no worries if you haven't had time yet. :)"

- **Meeting Etiquette**

    Arrive on time for meetings, prepared to contribute. During the meeting, pay attention, take notes, and avoid interrupting others. If you have questions or thoughts, wait for the appropriate moment to share them. If it's a virtual meeting, make sure your background is tidy and keep your microphone on mute when not speaking.

- **Professional Communication**

    How you speak to colleagues matters. Always be polite, even in casual conversations. Respect other people's time by keeping messages concise and relevant. If you need help or clarification, ask, but be mindful of how often you're asking for assistance—balance independence with seeking guidance.

Exercise 1: Professional Etiquette Checklist

Create a checklist of dos and don'ts for workplace communication, meetings, and email etiquette. Review it before important interactions to keep your behaviour on point.

Navigating Social Dynamics

Workplaces aren't just about work—they're social environments, too. Building good relationships with colleagues can make your job more enjoyable and help you succeed. But fitting in socially doesn't mean losing your authenticity. Here's how to navigate workplace dynamics:

- **Joining Workplace Conversations**

    It's easy to feel like an outsider when you first start, but don't be afraid to join in workplace conversations. Start with small talk—ask people how their weekend was or comment on something neutral, like the weather. Gradually, you'll become part of the regular office banter.

- **The Power of Listening**

    Listening is one of the most valuable social skills. Pay attention to what your colleagues are saying and show genuine interest. Don't just wait for your turn to speak—ask follow-up questions or offer encouragement. Listening helps you build deeper connections.

- **Understanding Unwritten Rules**

    Every workplace has unwritten rules—things that aren't in the handbook but are widely accepted. For example, you might notice that certain people always sit in the same seats during meetings, or there's a shared understanding about when it's okay to take a longer lunch. Observing and respecting these nuances helps you integrate smoothly.

Exercise 2: Networking Practice

Attend a networking event or a social gathering. Set a goal to introduce yourself to at least three new people. Reflect on the experience afterward—what worked, what didn't, and how you felt.

Fitting In While Staying Authentic

It's important to adapt to your new environment, but that doesn't mean you should change who you are. Finding the balance between fitting in and staying authentic is key to feeling comfortable at work.

- **Be Yourself (Within Reason)**

    While you want to adapt to your company's culture, it's important to bring your personality to work. If you're naturally more introverted, that's okay—just be open and approachable. If you have a quirky sense of humour, share it when appropriate. Authenticity helps you build genuine relationships with colleagues.

- **Respect Diversity**

    Workplaces are full of people with different backgrounds, beliefs, and experiences. Be respectful and open-minded and avoid making assumptions or judgments. Celebrate diversity by learning from others and contributing your unique perspective.

Handling Office Politics

Office politics are an inevitable part of most workplaces, and while it's not always pleasant, understanding how to navigate it is essential for your success.

- **Build Trust**

    Building trust with your colleagues is the best way to avoid being pulled into office politics. Be reliable, keep your word, and maintain professionalism in your interactions. People who trust you are less likely to involve you in petty disputes or gossip.

- **Stay Neutral**

    If you find yourself caught between colleagues with differing opinions, try to stay neutral. Avoid taking sides or getting involved in conflicts that don't directly affect you. Focus on your work, and when possible, encourage collaboration and problem-solving rather than division.

- **Pick Your Battles**

    Sometimes you'll need to stand up for yourself or your ideas, but it's important to choose your battles wisely. Not every disagreement is worth escalating, so evaluate the situation before deciding to speak up or let it go.

Receiving and Using Feedback

Learning how to receive feedback is one of the most important skills for personal and professional growth.

- **Embrace Constructive Criticism**

    Feedback is part of every job, and it's meant to help you grow. Instead of getting defensive, try to understand the feedback and think about how you can apply it. Ask clarifying questions if needed and show that you're open to improving.

- **Turn Feedback into Action**

    After receiving feedback, create an action plan to address the areas of improvement. For example, if you're told that your communication could be clearer, make a point to slow down and organise your thoughts before speaking or writing.

Exercise 3: Feedback Reflection

After receiving feedback, write down the key points. Identify at least one specific action you will take to improve based on this feedback. Set a timeline for when you'll check in on your progress.

Chapter 12 Summary

Fitting into a new workplace can be intimidating, but with the right social skills and etiquette, you'll be able to navigate your environment with confidence. Remember:

- **First impressions matter**, so start off on the right foot with proper introductions, professional dress, and a positive attitude.
- **Workplace etiquette**—from email to meetings—is essential for maintaining professionalism.
- **Navigating social dynamics** takes time, but listening, observing unwritten rules, and joining conversations help you fit in smoothly.
- **Stay authentic** while respecting the company culture and embracing diversity.
- **Handle office politics** with care by staying neutral, building trust, and picking your battles.
- **Use feedback** as a tool for growth, not criticism.

With these tools in hand, you'll be well-equipped to thrive in the social side of the workplace while staying true to yourself.

Chapter 13: How to Keep Growing in Your Career

Congratulations! You've started your career and made it through the initial learning curve. But now the question is, how do you continue to grow? Many people think career growth stops after they land their first job, but that's far from the truth. Career growth is an ongoing process that helps you stay engaged, fulfilled, and continuously moving forward.

In this chapter, we'll dive into why growth is essential, how to seek out new challenges, and practical steps you can take to ensure you're always developing new skills and expanding your horizons.

Why Career Growth is Important

Career growth doesn't just happen—it requires intentional effort. If you're not actively seeking new opportunities to learn, you risk stagnating and losing motivation. Growth is key to staying competitive in the job market, feeling fulfilled at work, and positioning yourself for future promotions or career shifts.

Let's break down a few reasons why career growth is important:

- **Staying Engaged**

    If you're not learning or facing new challenges, boredom sets in. Continuous growth keeps you engaged and excited about your work.

- **Remaining Relevant**

    Industries change, technology evolves, and new skills become necessary. Actively growing in your career ensures you stay relevant and up to date with the latest trends.

- **Preparing for Future Opportunities**

    The more you grow, the more prepared you'll be when new opportunities arise—whether it's a promotion, a career shift, or a completely new field.

Growth is essential if you want to stay engaged and fulfilled in your work. It's not just about getting promotions or making more money (though those things can be nice). It's about feeling challenged, learning new things, and building a career that continues to excite and inspire you.

How to Keep Growing in Your Career

Growth doesn't have to mean going back to school or taking on overwhelming projects. Small, manageable steps can help you continually progress. Here's how to stay on track:

- **Take on Stretch Assignments**

    A stretch assignment is a project that pushes you beyond your current skill set. It might feel uncomfortable at first, but these assignments help you grow faster. You'll learn new skills, build confidence, and show your manager that you're ready for more responsibility.

- **Seek Feedback Regularly**

    Feedback is one of the most valuable tools for growth. Ask for feedback regularly from your manager, peers, or even mentors. Be open to constructive criticism—it's the best way to identify areas for improvement and take action.

- **Stay Curious and Learn Continuously**

    Commit to lifelong learning. Whether it's through online courses, podcasts, books, or workshops, there's always something new to discover. Platforms like Coursera, Udemy, and LinkedIn Learning offer endless opportunities to develop new skills at your own pace.

- **Find a Mentor**

    Having a mentor can accelerate your growth. A mentor provides guidance, shares their experiences, and offers advice on how to navigate challenges. If you don't have a mentor, consider reaching out to someone you admire in your field and asking if they'd be open to meeting for regular check-ins.

- **Build Your Network**

    Networking isn't just for job searching—it's a great way to grow in your current role. Connecting with people in your industry can help you stay informed about trends, discover new opportunities, and even get insights on how others are growing their careers.

Exercise 1: Setting Career Growth Goals

Let's start by setting some career growth goals. Take a moment to reflect on where you are in your career and where you want to go. Use these questions to guide your goal setting:

- **What skills do you want to develop in the next 6 months?**

    Think about both technical skills and soft skills (like leadership, communication, or time management). Choose 2-3 areas to focus on.

- **What new responsibilities could you take on?**

    Is there a project or task you've been interested in that you haven't had a chance to try yet? Look for opportunities to stretch yourself.

- **Where do you want to be in a year?**

    This isn't about having a rigid plan, but it's helpful to have a sense of direction. Do you want to be in the same role, or are you aiming for a promotion or new job?

Once you've set your goals, break them down into smaller, actionable steps, and review your progress monthly to stay on track. This will help you stay focused on your growth.

How to Track Your Growth

It's important to track your career growth so you can see how far you've come. Here are a few ways to measure progress:

- **Keep a Journal**

    Document the new skills you're learning, feedback you've received, and challenges you've overcome. This will help you reflect on your growth over time.

- **Ask for Progress Reviews**

    If possible, schedule quarterly or biannual progress reviews with your manager. This gives you the opportunity to get formal feedback, discuss areas for growth, and outline your future career goals.

- **Track Your Achievements**

    Keep a running list of your accomplishments and new skills. This will come in handy when updating your CV or preparing for performance reviews or job applications.

The Power of Mentorship

One of the most valuable tools for career growth is mentorship. Having someone who has walked the path before you, who can offer guidance and advice, is incredibly beneficial. A mentor can help you see your blind spots, navigate challenges, and offer support as you grow.

Here's how to find a mentor:

- **Look for someone you admire.**

    This could be someone in your company, a former professor, or even someone in your network who has experience in your field.

- **Reach out.**

    Don't be afraid to ask for mentorship. Most people are happy to share their knowledge and help others grow. Start with a simple message, asking if they'd be willing to meet for a coffee or chat to offer some career advice.

- **Build a relationship.**

    Mentorship isn't a one-time thing. It's a relationship that grows over time. Be open to feedback, ask questions, and keep in touch regularly.

Exercise 2: Creating Your Growth Action Plan

Let's make an action plan to keep your growth on track. Answer these questions to guide your next steps:

- **What skill do I want to improve most right now?**

    Is there something you've been struggling with or an area where you feel weak? Choose one specific skill to focus on for the next few months.

- **What project or responsibility can I take on to grow this skill?**

    Look for opportunities at work that will challenge this skill. If nothing comes to mind, talk to your manager about projects you're interested in.

- **Who can help me grow?**

    Identify mentors, colleagues, or managers who can offer advice, feedback, or opportunities for growth. Don't hesitate to ask for guidance.

- **How will I track my progress?**

    Decide how often you'll review your progress and adjust your goals. This could be a monthly review of your growth journal or check-ins with your manager.

Chapter 13 Summary

In summary, career growth is an ongoing process that requires intentional effort. It's easy to become comfortable once you've settled into your job, but actively seeking new challenges and learning opportunities keeps you engaged and helps you prepare for the future.

Let's recap:

- **Take on stretch assignments** to push your limits and develop new skills.

- **Seek feedback regularly** to identify areas for improvement and take action.
- **Stay curious** and commit to continuous learning through courses, books, and workshops.
- **Find a mentor** to guide you through your career journey.
- **Track your progress** through journaling, achievements, and regular reviews.

Remember, growth doesn't have to be overwhelming—it's about small, consistent steps that add up over time. As you continue your career, keep asking yourself: How can I keep growing, and how can I stay excited about what's ahead?

Chapter 14: Finding Balance and Avoiding Burnout

While growing in your career is important, it's equally important to find balance and protect your mental and emotional well-being. If you're always pushing yourself to achieve more without taking care of yourself, burnout can creep in—and that's something you want to avoid.

In this chapter, we'll talk about how to find balance between your ambition and your need for rest, how to recognise the signs of burnout, and how to set boundaries at work so you don't lose yourself in the process.

Why Work-Life Balance is Essential

Work-life balance isn't just a trendy concept—it's critical for long-term success and happiness. Without it, work can start to dominate your life, leaving little room for personal activities, hobbies, and relaxation. Over time, this imbalance can lead to stress, burnout, and even physical health issues.

Here are a few reasons why maintaining balance is so important:

- **Increased Productivity**

    Taking regular breaks and setting clear boundaries between work and personal time actually improves productivity. When you're well-rested, you're more focused, efficient, and able to handle challenges better.

- **Better Mental Health**

    Constant stress from overwork can lead to anxiety, depression, and other mental health issues. Prioritising balance allows you to recharge, reducing stress and boosting overall mental well-being.

- **Stronger Relationships**

    Maintaining balance means you'll have time to nurture relationships with family, friends, and loved ones. Strong personal connections are essential for happiness and help you cope with life's challenges.

How to Set Boundaries at Work

Setting boundaries is one of the most effective ways to create balance between your professional and personal life. Without clear boundaries, work can easily spill over into evenings, weekends, or even vacation time. Here's how to set healthy boundaries:

- **Set a Defined Work Schedule**

    Whether you're working remotely or in an office, set clear start and end times for your workday. Once you're done for the day, avoid checking emails or logging back in to finish tasks. Having a set schedule helps you mentally switch off from work.

- **Prioritise Your Tasks**

    Not every task is urgent. Learn to prioritise your work by focusing on what's most important, and delegate or delay non-urgent tasks. This reduces the pressure to "do it all" and helps you manage your workload more effectively.

- **Learn to Say No (When Necessary)**

    It can be tempting to say yes to every new project or request that comes your way, especially if you're eager to impress. But overcommitting yourself can lead to burnout. Practice saying no or negotiating deadlines to avoid taking on too much at once.

- **Use Breaks Wisely**

    Don't skip lunch or power through without taking breaks. Use break times to recharge—whether that's going for a walk, grabbing coffee, or simply stepping away from your desk to clear your mind.

Exercise 1: Assess Your Work-Life Balance

Take a moment to assess your current work-life balance. Are you making enough time for rest and play, or are you constantly in "work mode"? Use these prompts to reflect:

- **How many hours a week do I spend working?**

  This includes not only time at the office but also time spent checking emails or thinking about work outside of work hours.

- **How do I feel at the end of the workday?**

  Do you feel drained and exhausted, or do you feel energised and ready to enjoy your free time?

- **What activities am I missing out on because of work?**

  Are there hobbies, events, or personal relationships that are suffering because you're spending too much time working?

- **When does your workday typically start and end?**

  Are you sticking to these times, or do you find yourself working late into the evening?

- **What tasks are taking up too much of your time?**

  Identify non-essential tasks that could be delegated, delayed, or even eliminated from your to-do list.

- **How often do you take breaks?**

  Are you giving yourself enough time throughout the day to rest and recharge?

Once you've reflected, think about where you can make small adjustments to improve your balance.

Recognising the Signs of Burnout

Burnout doesn't happen overnight—it creeps in slowly. That's why it's important to recognise the signs early, so you can take action before things get worse. Here are some common signs of burnout:

- **Chronic Fatigue:** Feeling tired all the time, even after a good night's sleep.
- **Lack of Motivation:** Struggling to find the energy or enthusiasm for tasks you used to enjoy.
- **Irritability:** Becoming easily frustrated or upset over small things.
- **Decreased Productivity:** Finding it harder to focus and get things done.
- **Physical Symptoms:** Headaches, stomach aches, or other physical symptoms that seem stress related.

If you recognise any of these signs in yourself, it's time to take action before burnout becomes severe. Here are a few strategies to help prevent burnout:

- **Take Time Off**

    Don't be afraid to use your vacation days or take a mental health day when needed. Time away from work allows you to reset and return with renewed energy.

- **Set Realistic Expectations**

    Don't set impossible standards for yourself. It's okay to aim high but be realistic about what can be achieved within a given timeframe. If your workload is too heavy, communicate with your manager to adjust expectations.

- **Build in Time for Hobbies and Socialising**

    Prioritise activities outside of work that bring you joy, whether it's spending time with loved ones, engaging in hobbies, or simply relaxing. These activities help balance your life and provide mental refreshment.

Exercise 2: Creating a Balance Plan

Let's create a simple plan to help you maintain balance and avoid burnout. Answer the following:

- **What signs of burnout have you noticed in yourself recently?**

    Be honest about any signs of fatigue, stress, or lack of motivation that you've been experiencing.

- **How can you adjust your workload or schedule to reduce stress?**

    Consider delegating tasks, requesting extensions, or cutting back on non-essential projects.

- **What can I do to protect my personal time?**

    This could mean setting firmer boundaries with work or scheduling time each week for activities you enjoy.

- **How will I make sure I get enough rest?**

    Consider your sleep schedule, your breaks during the workday, and how you can incorporate rest into your routine.

- **What activities will I prioritise outside of work?**

    Make a list of the hobbies, interests, or social activities that bring you joy, and commit to making time for them.

By setting these intentions, you'll be better equipped to maintain a healthy work-life balance.

Chapter 14 Summary

Maintaining balance and avoiding burnout is essential to building a sustainable, fulfilling career. It's easy to get caught up in work, but without balance, you risk burnout, decreased productivity, and poor mental health. By setting clear boundaries, taking time for yourself, and recognising the signs of burnout early, you can create a career that not only challenges you but also supports your well-being.

Let's recap:

- **Set boundaries** at work by defining your work hours, saying no when necessary, and taking regular breaks.

- **Recognise the early signs of burnout** so you can take action before it gets worse.
- **Prioritise activities outside of work** to help recharge your mental and emotional energy.
- **Create a balance plan** to ensure you're staying on track and maintaining your well-being.

Remember, a successful career is about more than just work—it's about maintaining a healthy balance between professional growth and personal well-being. In the next part of the book, we'll explore how to navigate career changes or unexpected curveballs with confidence and resilience.

Part 4 Summary: Thriving in the Workplace (And Beyond)

You've come a long way! Part 4 has been all about navigating your new career and ensuring that you're not just surviving but thriving in the workplace—and beyond. Let's quickly recap what we've covered:

- **Starting Strong in Your First Job**

    In Chapter 11, we talked about how to make a great first impression, navigate workplace culture, and set yourself up for success in your first few weeks on the job.

- **Mastering Workplace Social Skills and Etiquette**

    In Chapter 12, we looked at how workplace etiquette, social dynamics, fitting in while still staying authentic, office politics and feedback. Fitting into a new workplace can be intimidating, but with the right social skills and etiquette, you'll be able to navigate your environment with confidence.

- **Continuing to Grow**

    In Chapter 13, we explored the importance of ongoing career growth—whether through new responsibilities, skill-building, or mentorship. Growth is a lifelong process, and it's up to you to seek out opportunities to keep evolving.

- **Finding Balance and Avoiding Burnout**

    Chapter 14 focused on the importance of maintaining balance in your life. Career success is great, but it's not worth sacrificing your well-being. Setting boundaries and prioritising rest and joy are key to avoiding burnout and staying happy in your work.

Looking Ahead: What's Next?

As you continue your career journey, remember that it's a marathon, not a sprint. You'll have times of growth and challenge, and times when you need to rest and recharge. The key is to stay proactive, curious, and mindful of your well-being.

In the final section, we'll wrap up everything you've learned and give you the tools to stay adaptable and resilient as you move forward in your career and life. The future is full of possibilities—let's make sure you're ready for whatever comes your way.

Part 5 Introduction: Career Change or Curveball? That's Okay Too!

Life rarely goes exactly as planned, and that includes your career. You might find yourself wanting to change directions after a few years in a particular job, or maybe something unexpected happens—like a job loss, a personal challenge, or even a global pandemic—that forces you to rethink your path. In Part 5, we're going to explore how to navigate these career shifts with confidence and resilience. Whether you're choosing to make a change, or life has thrown you a curveball, this section will help you see that change isn't something to be feared. It's an opportunity to grow, reinvent yourself, and find new possibilities.

We'll talk about recognising when it's time to make a change, how to pivot into a new field, and how to handle those unexpected challenges that inevitably pop up along the way. Change is part of life—and with the right mindset and tools, you can navigate it with grace and come out stronger on the other side.

Chapter 15: When You Want to Change Your Career (And Don't Know How)

At some point in your career, you might find yourself thinking, "Is this really what I want to be doing?" Maybe you've been in the same role for a few years, and it's starting to feel routine. Or perhaps you've discovered new interests that make you wonder if you're on the right path. This is completely normal. Most people go through career shifts multiple times in their lives, and making a change can be one of the most rewarding decisions you'll ever make.

But knowing that you want to change and knowing *how* to change are two different things. In this chapter, we'll explore how to recognise when it's time for a change, how to pivot into something new, and how to make sure your career change aligns with who you are and what you want.

How to Know When It's Time for a Change

It's easy to feel uncertain about whether you should stick it out in your current role or take the leap into something new. The fear of the unknown often keeps us in jobs that no longer challenge or fulfil us. So how do you know when it's time to make a change? Here are a few signs that might help you decide:

- **You're No Longer Learning**

    If you feel like you're just going through the motions at work without learning anything new, it could be a sign that you've outgrown your role. When there's no room for growth or development, it's hard to stay motivated.

- **You're Constantly Drained**

    Everyone has stressful days, but if you're feeling mentally and emotionally drained most of the time, it could be a sign that the job is no longer right for you. When work feels like a chore rather than a source of fulfilment, it might be time to explore other options.

- **Your Values Have Shifted**

    Over time, your personal values may evolve, and what you once found important may no longer align with the work you're doing. Maybe you've discovered a passion for sustainability, creativity, or helping others, and your current job doesn't support those values.

- **You're Daydreaming About Other Careers**

    If you find yourself frequently fantasising about different careers or industries, that's a sign that your interests may be shifting. Those daydreams could be pointing you toward a career path that better aligns with who you are today.

Exercise 1: Career Reflection

If you're feeling unsure about whether it's time for a career change, take some time to reflect on the following questions:

- **What do I enjoy most about my current job?**

    Are there aspects of your role that you still enjoy, or do you struggle to find things that excite you?

- **What frustrates me about my current job?**

    Identify the things that drain you or make you unhappy. Are they fixable, or are they core aspects of the role?

- **What skills or interests have I developed recently?**

    Have you discovered new passions or talents that aren't being used in your current role?

- **How do I feel about staying in this role for another year?**

    If the thought of staying in your current job for another year feels heavy or uninspiring, it might be time to consider a change.

Use these reflections to get clarity on whether a career shift is the right move for you.

How to Make a Career Change (Without Starting Over)

One of the biggest fears about changing careers is the idea that you'll have to start over from scratch. But here's the good news: you don't. Even if you're moving into a completely different field, the skills and experiences you've gained are valuable. You're not starting from zero—you're building on what you already know.

Here's how to make a career change without feeling like you're going back to square one:

- **Identify Transferable Skills**

    Every job teaches you skills that can be applied elsewhere. Think about the skills you've developed in your current role—communication, project management, problem-solving, leadership. These are all valuable in many industries. Focus on highlighting these transferable skills as you make your move.

- **Learn New Skills (Without Going Back to School)**

    If your new career requires specific skills that you don't have yet, don't worry. You don't necessarily need to go back to school for a new degree. There are plenty of online courses, workshops, and certifications that can help you gain the knowledge you need in a short amount of time.

- **Leverage Your Network**

    Networking is crucial when making a career change. Reach out to people in the field you're interested in, ask for informational interviews, and get advice on how to make the transition. Often, a referral or recommendation from someone in the industry can help open doors.

- **Start Small**

    If you're not ready to make a full leap into a new career, consider starting small. You could take on freelance work, volunteer, or start a side project that lets you explore your new field while maintaining your current job. This gives you the chance to test the waters before making a full commitment.

Exercise 2: Transferable Skills Inventory

To help you make a smooth career transition, let's start by identifying your transferable skills. Think about your current role, as well as any previous jobs or projects you've worked on. Write down the skills you've developed that can apply to other fields. Here are a few categories to get you started:

- **Communication:** Are you good at presenting ideas, writing reports, or leading meetings?
- **Problem-Solving:** Have you tackled complex challenges or found solutions to difficult problems?
- **Teamwork and Leadership:** Have you managed a team, led a project, or collaborated with others to achieve a goal?
- **Project Management:** Are you experienced in organising tasks, managing timelines, and delivering results?
- **Technical Skills:** Do you have expertise in specific tools, software, or processes that can be applied in a different industry?

Once you've identified your transferable skills, think about how you can highlight these in your job search.

How to Overcome the Fear of Change

Change can be scary, especially when it comes to something as important as your career. But staying in a job that no longer fulfils you can be even scarier. Here are some tips to help you overcome the fear of change:

- **Take Small Steps**

    You don't have to make a huge leap all at once. Break the process into smaller, manageable steps, like updating your CV, taking a course, or reaching out to someone in your network. Each step will build your confidence and reduce the fear.

- **Focus on the Positive**

    Instead of focusing on what you're leaving behind, think about the exciting possibilities ahead. What new skills will you learn? What new challenges will you tackle? What new opportunities are waiting for you?

- **Trust Yourself**

    You've made career moves before, and you can do it again. Trust that you have the skills, resilience, and adaptability to succeed in whatever path you choose.

Chapter 15 Summary

Here's what we covered:

- Recognising when it's time to make a career change, whether because you're no longer growing, feeling drained, or your values have shifted.

- How to make a career change without starting from scratch, by leveraging your transferable skills and gaining new knowledge through small steps.

- Overcoming the fear of change by taking things one step at a time and focusing on the positive opportunities ahead.

Making a career change can feel daunting, but it's also an opportunity to reinvent yourself and find a path that's more aligned with who you are today. In the next chapter, we'll talk about how to handle unexpected curveballs in your career—because sometimes life has other plans, and that's okay too.

Chapter 16: Handling Career Curveballs (And Bouncing Back)

Sometimes, life throws you a curveball—something unexpected that shakes up your career plans. Maybe it's a job loss, an economic downturn, a personal challenge, or a global event that disrupts your industry. Whatever the curveball, it can feel overwhelming and even scary when your career path suddenly changes. But here's the thing: setbacks are part of life, and how you respond to them can determine what comes next.

In this chapter, we'll talk about how to handle those unexpected moments in your career, how to bounce back, and how to use these challenges as opportunities to grow. No matter what life throws your way, you have the resilience and ability to navigate it—and come out stronger on the other side.

How to Manage Career Setbacks

When a career setback hits, whether it's losing your job, missing out on a promotion, or facing an industry shift, it can be tough to see the silver lining. But setbacks aren't the end of your career—they're just a bump in the road. Here's how to manage these moments:

- **Give Yourself Time to Process**

    It's okay to feel frustrated, disappointed, or even angry when something unexpected happens. Give yourself permission to feel those emotions, but don't let them take over. Once you've had time to process, you can start thinking about your next steps.

- **Take Stock of What You've Learned**

    Every setback is an opportunity to learn. Whether it's a job loss or a missed opportunity, reflect on what the experience taught you. Did you gain new skills? Did you learn how to handle challenges? These lessons will be valuable as you move forward.

- **Create a Plan for Moving Forward**

    Once you've processed the setback, it's time to create a plan. This might involve updating your CV, reaching out to your network, or looking for opportunities in a new field. Breaking things down into small, manageable steps makes the situation feel less overwhelming.

Exercise 1: Reframing a Setback

Think about a career setback you've experienced—whether it's a job loss, a missed opportunity, or something that felt like a step backward. Take a moment to reframe that experience by answering these questions:

- **What did I learn from this experience?**

    What skills or insights did you gain, even if the outcome wasn't what you wanted?

- **How can I use this experience to grow?**

    How will this challenge make you more resilient, adaptable, or skilled moving forward?

- **What are my next steps?**

    What's the first action you can take to move past the setback? Whether it's updating your LinkedIn profile, reaching out to a mentor, or starting a job search, taking action helps shift your focus from what went wrong to what's possible next.

How to Pivot After a Job Loss

Losing a job can feel like a major blow, but it's not the end of the world. In fact, many people look back on job losses as turning points that led them to more fulfilling careers. If you're facing a job loss, here's how to handle it with resilience:

- **Update Your Skills**

    Take advantage of this time to build new skills or gain certifications that will make you more competitive in the job market. Online courses, workshops, and webinars are great ways to stay productive and prepare for your next opportunity.

- **Leverage Your Network**

    Don't be afraid to let people know that you're looking for new opportunities. Reach out to former colleagues, mentors, and friends. Often, job leads come from people in your network who know about opportunities before they're advertised.

- **Stay Open to New Opportunities**

    A job loss might be the perfect opportunity to pivot into a new industry or role that better aligns with your passions and skills. Stay open to different possibilities, even if they weren't part of your original career plan.

How to Stay Resilient in Times of Uncertainty

When the world feels uncertain—whether because of economic changes, industry shifts, or personal challenges—it's easy to feel stuck. But resilience is about adapting to change and staying flexible. Here's how to build resilience in your career:

- **Stay Adaptable**

    The ability to adapt is one of the most valuable skills you can have in today's fast-changing world. Be open to learning new skills, taking on different roles, or exploring new industries. The more adaptable you are, the easier it is to navigate uncertainty.

- **Focus on What You Can Control**

    In times of uncertainty, it's easy to feel powerless. Instead of worrying about things outside your control (like economic downturns or industry disruptions), focus on what you *can* control—your attitude, your actions, and your willingness to learn and grow.

- **Take Care of Yourself**

    Resilience isn't just about your career—it's also about your mental and emotional well-being. During times of uncertainty, make sure you're taking care of yourself by maintaining a healthy work-life balance, staying connected with loved ones, and practicing self-care.

Exercise 2: Building Your Resilience

Let's practice building resilience by reflecting on a time when you faced uncertainty. Use these prompts to guide your reflection:

- What was the challenge or uncertainty you faced? Describe the situation and how it affected you.
- How did you adapt? What steps did you take to manage the uncertainty and keep moving forward?
- What strengths do you rely on? Did you draw on any particular skills or personal qualities to help you through the challenge?
- What did you learn from the experience? Reflect on the lessons you learned and how they have made you more resilient today.

By focusing on your past experiences, you'll remind yourself that you've handled uncertainty before—and you can do it again.

Chapter 16 Summary

- How to handle career setbacks by giving yourself time to process, learning from the experience, and creating a plan for moving forward.
- How to pivot after a job loss by updating your skills, leveraging your network, and staying open to new opportunities.
- Building resilience by staying adaptable, focusing on what you can control, and taking care of your mental and emotional well-being.

Career curveballs are never easy, but they're a part of life. The key is to stay resilient, stay open, and trust that every challenge is an opportunity for growth. In the next section, we'll wrap up everything we've covered and give you the tools to stay adaptable and successful, no matter what your career journey brings.

Chapter 17: The Future of Work

The world of work is constantly evolving, and the pace of change is only accelerating. With advances in technology, shifting industries, and new ways of working, it's essential to stay ahead of the curve. But don't worry—these changes aren't something to fear. Instead, they offer opportunities to grow, adapt, and build a future-proof career.

In this chapter, we'll explore the key trends shaping the future of work, how to prepare for these changes, and the skills you'll need to thrive in the new world of work.

Embrace Lifelong Learning

In the past, people learned a skill or trade, got a job, and stuck with it for decades. But today, the idea of "one job for life" is outdated. With industries and technologies evolving rapidly, the most successful professionals are those who commit to **lifelong learning**.

- **Why Lifelong Learning Matters**

    Continuous learning keeps your skills relevant and ensures you stay competitive in the job market. Whether it's mastering new software, developing leadership skills, or staying updated on industry trends, learning never stops.

- **How to Stay Current**

    Take advantage of online courses, workshops, and industry events. Platforms like **Coursera**, **edX**, and **Udemy** offer affordable and accessible learning opportunities for a wide range of subjects. Don't just wait for formal training—seek out learning opportunities on your own.

- **Learning on the Job**

    Look for ways to grow within your current role. Ask for projects that challenge you or expose you to new skills. If your company offers internal training or mentorship programs, sign up! The more you learn, the more valuable you become.

Technology and Automation: A Friend, Not a Foe

One of the biggest drivers of change in the workplace is technology. Automation, artificial intelligence (AI), and robotics are transforming industries, but this doesn't mean robots are coming for your job. Instead, technology is changing how we work—and often making it easier.

- **Automation and AI**

    Automation can take over repetitive tasks, allowing you to focus on more complex and creative work. For example, AI might handle data entry or customer service queries, freeing you up for strategic thinking and innovation.

- **Developing Tech-Savvy Skills**

    To thrive in the future of work, it's important to stay **tech-savvy**. You don't have to be a coder, but understanding basic technology, data literacy, and digital tools is essential. Take time to learn new software, keep up with tech trends, and be open to using technology to improve your work.

- **Human Skills Still Matter**

    While technology can handle many tasks, it can't replace human creativity, empathy, or leadership. These skills—sometimes called "soft skills"—will always be in demand. Focus on developing your problem-solving, communication, and emotional intelligence to stay valuable in a tech-driven world.

Remote Work and Flexibility: The New Normal

The COVID-19 pandemic accelerated the shift to remote work, and many companies are embracing flexible work models permanently. Whether you work from home full-time, part-time, or on a hybrid schedule, understanding how to succeed in a remote environment is crucial.

- **Mastering Remote Work**

    Working from home requires discipline and good time management. Create a dedicated workspace, set clear work hours, and minimise distractions to stay productive. Use tools like **Slack**, **Zoom**, or **Trello** to stay connected with your team and manage your tasks effectively.

- **Maintaining Work-Life Balance**

    Flexibility is one of the perks of remote work, but it can also blur the lines between work and personal life. Set boundaries—turn off work notifications after hours and make time for breaks during the day. Finding balance is key to avoiding burnout.

- **Adaptability is Key**

    Whether working remotely or in-person, flexibility is becoming a hallmark of modern careers. Be adaptable—embrace change and be open to shifting roles, projects, and even industries as needed.

Building Your Network in the Future of Work

Networking has always been important, but as the future of work evolves, it's becoming even more critical. The days of handing out business cards at conferences might be fading, but building strong connections—both online and in person—remains essential.

- **Online Networking**

    Platforms like **LinkedIn** are invaluable for building professional connections. Keep your profile updated, engage with content in your field, and don't be afraid to reach out to new contacts for informational interviews or advice.

- **Nurturing Relationships**

    Networking isn't just about making new connections—it's about maintaining them. Stay in touch with former colleagues, mentors, and industry peers. A simple "How are you?" message or sharing an interesting article can keep your relationships alive.

- **Networking in a Hybrid World**

    With remote and hybrid work models becoming the norm, digital networking skills are crucial. But don't forget the value of face-to-face interactions. Whenever possible, attend industry events, meetups, or conferences to build personal connections.

Preparing for Multiple Career Changes

In the future of work, it's likely you'll switch careers multiple times. This isn't something to be afraid of—it's an opportunity to explore new passions and industries. Here's how to stay ready for career shifts

- **Be Open to Change**

    Embrace career transitions as part of your professional journey. If your industry changes or you lose interest in your current field, view it as an opportunity to pivot into something new.

- **Transferable Skills are Key**

    Focus on building skills that transfer across industries, such as leadership, communication, and project management. These core competencies will serve you in any role.

- **Take Time to Reflect**

    Regularly reflect on where you are in your career and where you want to go. Don't be afraid to reassess your goals and make adjustments. Flexibility and adaptability will help you thrive in a world where career paths are less linear.

Chapter 17 Summary

The future of work is full of change, but it's also full of opportunities. Here's what to keep in mind:

- **Embrace lifelong learning** to stay relevant in your industry.
- **Stay tech-savvy** and develop skills that complement automation and AI.
- **Be adaptable**—remote work and flexible models are here to stay.
- **Build your network** both online and in person to stay connected.

- **Prepare for career shifts** by developing transferable skills and remaining open to change.

By staying flexible, curious, and committed to growth, you'll not only survive the future of work—you'll thrive in it. The key to success is adaptability, a willingness to learn, and the confidence to take risks and explore new opportunities.

Part 5 Summary: Career Change or Curveball? That's Okay Too!

Change is inevitable, both in life and in your career. Whether you're choosing to make a change, or life throws you a curveball, navigating these shifts with confidence is key to long-term success and fulfilment. Here's a recap of what we've covered in Part 5:

- **When You Want to Change Your Career**

    In Chapter 15, we talked about how to recognise when it's time for a career change and how to pivot into a new field without starting from scratch. By leveraging your transferable skills and staying open to learning, you can make a smooth transition.

- **Handling Career Curveballs**

    Chapter 16 focused on how to bounce back from unexpected setbacks, whether it's a job loss, industry shift, or personal challenge. Resilience is the key to navigating uncertainty, and staying adaptable will help you thrive in any situation.

- **The Future of Work**

    Chapter 17 looked ahead to the future of work. Embrace lifelong learning, stay tech-savvy, be adaptable, build your network and prepare for career shifts by developing transferable skills and remaining open to change. By staying flexible, curious, and committed to growth, you'll not only survive the future of work—you'll thrive in it.

Looking Ahead: What's Next?

You've made it through the ups and downs of career building, and you're well-equipped with the tools you need to succeed. In the final section, we'll tie everything together, helping you stay adaptable and focused as you move forward. Remember, your career is a journey—and with each step, you're growing, learning, and moving closer to the life you want.

Conclusion: Bringing It All Home

You've made it to the end of this journey, but in many ways, it's just the beginning. Throughout this book, we've covered a lot—everything from understanding who you are and what you want, to building the skills you need, landing your first job, and navigating the twists and turns that come along the way. Whether you're just starting out or you've already faced a few curveballs, you're now armed with the tools, mindset, and resilience to build a career—and life—that truly fits who you are.

Remember, It's a Journey, Not a Race

If there's one thing I want you to take away from this, it's that your career isn't a straight path with a finish line you have to cross by a certain age. It's a journey that will evolve over time. You'll grow, your interests will change, and you'll discover new things about yourself along the way. And that's okay—more than okay, actually. It's part of the adventure.

Success isn't about having everything figured out from day one. It's about staying curious, taking risks, and learning as you go. You don't need to have all the answers right now. What matters is that you're willing to take the next step, even if it feels uncertain.

Building Your Career, Step by Step

Here's a quick recap of the key steps we've covered:

- **Understanding Yourself**

    We started by helping you figure out who you are—your values, strengths, and what really drives you. This self-reflection is the foundation for making decisions that align with who you are, not what others expect from you.

- **Building Skills and Confidence**

    From identifying the skills you need to building confidence in your abilities, you've learned how to create a strong foundation that will carry you through your career. Skills aren't just technical—they include resilience, adaptability, and communication, all of which help you navigate the workplace and life in general.

- **Landing the Job**

    Writing a CV, acing interviews, and networking might have seemed daunting at first, but you now have a clear strategy for each. Remember, it's about presenting yourself authentically and confidently, while always being open to learning from each experience.

- **Thriving in the Workplace**

    Your first job is just the beginning. Building relationships, setting boundaries, and continuing to grow are key to staying engaged and fulfilled in your career. You've learned that thriving isn't just about success at work—it's about balance and well-being too.

- **Navigating Change and Setbacks**

    Whether it's a career change you choose or a curveball life throws your way, you've learned how to stay adaptable and resilient. Change can be intimidating, but it's also a chance to reinvent yourself and find new opportunities.

Your Career, Your Way

At the end of the day, your career is *yours*. No one else can walk this path for you. And while advice, mentors, and guidance can be helpful, you're the one who gets to decide what success looks like for you. Whether it's climbing the corporate ladder, starting your own business, or pursuing a creative passion, it's up to you to define your path.

As you move forward, trust yourself. Trust that you have the ability to figure things out, even when the road gets bumpy. Trust that mistakes are part of the process, and that each one is teaching you something valuable. And most importantly, trust that your unique path—however it twists and turns—will lead you to where you need to be.

Looking Ahead

So, where do you go from here? Wherever you want. Take everything you've learned and keep moving forward. Stay curious, stay open, and keep growing. You don't have to have all the answers now—or ever. But as long as you're willing to keep exploring, learning, and adapting, you'll be more than okay.

Here's to building a career (and life) that truly reflects who you are—one step, one lesson, and one opportunity at a time.

Hints and Tips

Part 1: Understanding Yourself and Your Career Path

Chapter 1: Who Are You?

- **Take your time with self-reflection.** Personality tests (like Myers-Briggs or StrengthsFinder) can provide valuable insights into your strengths and preferences.
- **Keep a journal to track your self-discovery journey.** It helps clarify thoughts over time.
- **Ask trusted friends or mentors for feedback** on your strengths and weaknesses.
- **Ask for Feedback.** Others can provide insights into your strengths you might not see yourself.
- **Don't Rush Self-Discovery.** Be patient—understanding yourself is a process that evolves.

Chapter 2: What Do You Really Want?

- **List your core values and non-negotiables** e.g., work-life balance, creativity.
- **Separate "should" from "want"** by evaluating if your career aspirations are influenced by external pressures.
- **Visualise Your Dream Job.** Picture your ideal day at work to clarify what truly matters to you.
- **Visualise your ideal workday**—what excites and fulfils you?

Chapter 3: Taking the Pressure Off

- **Break Big Goals into Steps.** Tackling smaller, achievable steps makes career planning less daunting.
- **Remember, It's Okay to Pivot.** Changing paths isn't failure—it's part of growth.

- **Celebrate Small Wins.** Acknowledge progress, no matter how minor, to maintain motivation.

Part 2: Practical Steps to Building Your Career

Chapter 4: How to Figure Out What You're Good At

- **Review Past Experiences** Look for patterns in past successes that reveal your strengths.
- **Seek New Experiences.** Try volunteering, freelance work, or hobbies to discover untapped talents.
- **Ask Trusted Friends for Input** Others may notice strengths you overlook.
- **Use online tools** like LinkedIn Skills Assessment to gauge your current abilities.

Chapter 5: Skills That Matter (and How to Get Them)

- **Follow Industry Trends.** Stay updated on what skills are most in demand.
- **Practice Soft Skills.** Communication, teamwork, and leadership skills are just as valuable as technical skills.
- **Take Advantage of Free Resources.** Websites like Coursera, edX, and LinkedIn Learning offer free or low-cost courses.
- **Check job postings** for skills in demand in your field and focus on learning those first.
- **Join industry groups or forums** to stay updated on emerging trends and skills.

Chapter 6: Why Making Mistakes is Part of the Plan

- **Reframe Mistakes as Learning.** View each mistake as an opportunity to improve.
- **Reflect after each mistake**—what went wrong, and what would you do differently next time?

- **Keep a 'Failure Journal'.** Document mistakes and the lessons learned from them.
- **Take Responsibility, Not Blame.** Acknowledge errors but don't let them define you.
- **Seek feedback** from mentors or peers on how to improve.

Chapter 7: Building Confidence Without Faking It

- **Prepare Thoroughly.** Confidence comes from preparation, whether for a presentation or new task.
- **Practice Positive Self-Talk.** Replace negative thoughts with affirmations of your skills and worth.
- **Visualise Success.** Picture yourself succeeding in a task to build mental resilience but also acknowledge that you can handle setbacks when they come.
- **Practice makes progress.** Try mock interviews or presentations to boost confidence.

Part 3: Landing the Job

Chapter 8: How to Write a CV That Gets Noticed

- **Customise your CV.** Taylor your CV for each job, focusing on relevant experiences and skills.
- **Quantify your achievements wherever possible.** For example, "Increased sales by 20%".
- **Use keywords from the job description** to improve your chances with applicant tracking systems (ATS).
- **Use Action Verbs.** Start bullet points with action words like "led," "developed," or "managed."
- **Keep It Simple.** Use a clean, professional format—avoid graphics or fancy fonts unless appropriate for the field.

Chapter 9: Acing the Interview

- **Practice the STAR Method.** Prepare responses to behavioural questions using Situation, Task, Action, and Result.
- **Research the Company.** Tailor your answers to show you understand the company's goals and culture.
- **Prepare Questions.** Asking insightful questions shows you're serious and well-prepared.

Chapter 10: Networking Without Feeling Awkward

- **Start with people you know.** Use your existing connections and ask for introductions to others in your field.
- **Engage with professionals online.** Use networks like LinkedIn and comment on their posts or sharing articles relevant to your industry. LinkedIn and professional groups are also great ways to network without the pressure of in-person events.
- **Quality Over Quantity.** Focus on building deeper relationships with a few key contacts.
- **Follow up.** Contact people you meet after networking events or meetings to keep relationships alive.

Part 4: Thriving in the Workplace (And Beyond)

Chapter 11: Starting Your First Job (And Doing It Well)

- **Ask lots of questions during your first weeks.** This shows initiative and eagerness to learn.
- **Establish a good relationship with your manager.** Have regular check-ins with your manager to align on your progress and expectations.
- **Observe and Adapt.** Pay attention to how colleagues interact and adjust your approach accordingly but stay true to your values.

Chapter 12: Mastering Workplace Social Skills and Etiquette

- **Smile and Be Approachable**. First impressions aren't just about appearance—your energy and friendliness count.

- **Start with Small Talk**. Don't overthink it—asking about someone's weekend or commenting on shared experiences builds rapport.

- **Be Prompt with Emails**. Respond to emails within 24 hours to show professionalism.

- **Meetings are for Listening Too**. Don't feel pressure to always contribute. Listening shows respect and understanding.

- **Balance Formality**. Adapt your tone depending on the culture of the office—keep emails professional until you know what's acceptable.

- **Build Genuine Connections**. Focus on quality interactions over quantity—be genuinely interested in your colleagues' lives.

- **Don't Be Afraid to Ask**. If you're unsure about workplace norms, ask a trusted colleague. It shows you care about fitting in.

- **Body Language Counts**: Pay attention to non-verbal cues like eye contact, nodding, and body posture to show engagement.

- **Stay Open to Feedback**. Accept that colleagues might help you understand unwritten rules—adjust as needed while staying true to yourself. If feedback is vague, ask for examples to better understand how to improve.

- **Avoid Gossip**. Keep personal conversations respectful and avoid workplace drama.

- **Build Trust Slowly**. Reliability and honesty will keep you out of the political fray.

Chapter 13: How to Keep Growing in Your Career

- **Choose Battles Wisely**. Don't engage in minor conflicts—stay focused on what's important.

- **Embrace Criticism**. See feedback as a tool for growth, not a personal attack.

- **Make Feedback Actionable**. Turn feedback into clear, actionable steps. Show progress when you get feedback again.
- **Schedule regular skill assessments.** Identify growth areas every few months.
- **Volunteer for stretch assignments or projects** to challenge yourself and grow.
- **Find a mentor** to guide your career development and offer advice.

Chapter 14: Finding Balance and Avoiding Burnout

- **Set Boundaries**. Define clear work hours and stick to them—avoid overextending yourself.
- **Prioritise Self-Care**. Physical exercise, hobbies, and downtime are essential for avoiding burnout.
- **Learn to Say No**. Be selective about additional responsibilities; don't overload yourself with tasks.
- **Take Regular Breaks**. Step away from work during the day to recharge and reset your focus.

Part 5: Career Change or Curveball? That's Okay Too!

Chapter 15: When You Want to Change Your Career (And Don't Know How)

- **Identify Transferable Skills**. Focus on skills you can bring into a new field, such as leadership, communication, or problem-solving.
- **Start Small**. Explore new careers through side projects, freelancing, taking online courses, attending workshops or volunteering before making a full leap.
- **Research Industries**. Deep dive into fields you're interested in to understand the demands, expectations, and opportunities.
- **Leverage Your Network**. Reach out to contacts for advice, informational interviews, or potential job leads.

Chapter 16: Handling Career Curveballs (And Bouncing Back)

- **Accept the Setback**. Give yourself time to process, but don't dwell on the past—focus on what's next.
- **Update Your Skills**. Use downtime to enrol in courses, workshops, or training that will help you stay competitive.
- **Stay Open to New Opportunities**. Be flexible—sometimes a career detour can lead to unexpected but rewarding opportunities.
- **Build Resilience**. Reflect on past challenges you've overcome to remind yourself of your adaptability and strength.
- **Reframe unexpected events.** See them as opportunities to learn or pivot in a new direction.
- **Keep your network warm, even when not actively job-hunting.** Support is invaluable when things change suddenly.

Chapter 17: The Future of Work

- **Embrace Lifelong Learning.** In a rapidly evolving job market, continuously updating your skills is crucial.
- **Stay Tech-Savvy.** Keep up with emerging technologies and tools relevant to your field.
- **Adaptability is Key.** Be ready to pivot as industries change—flexibility will ensure long-term success.
- **Network Regularly.** Keep your network warm, even when you're not job-hunting—relationships are critical for career growth in the future of work.

Resources

Part 1: Understanding Yourself and Your Career Path
Chapter 1: Who Are You?

- Myers-Briggs Personality Test (MBTI): Helps you understand your personality type and strengths. Free personality test, type descriptions, relationship and career advice | 16Personalities (https://www.16personalities.com/)

- StrengthsFinder: Discover your natural talents through Gallup's CliftonStrengths assessment. CliftonStrengths Online Talent Assessment | EN - Gallup(https://www.gallup.com)

Chapter 2: What Do You Really Want?

- Ikigai Framework: Japanese concept for discovering your purpose. The Philosophy of Ikigai: 3 Examples About Finding Purpose(https://www.positivephyscology.com)

- MindTools Values Test: Identify your core values to align your career with them. MindTools | Home(www.mindtools.com)

Chapter 3: Taking the Pressure Off

- Calm App: Meditation and mindfulness exercises to help reduce career-related stress. Calm - The #1 App for Meditation and Sleep(https://www.calm.com)

- TED Talk: The Power of Vulnerability by Brené Brown: A great resource on how vulnerability leads to growth and resilience. Calm - The #1 App for Meditation and Sleep(https://www.calm.com)

Part 2: Practical Steps to Building Your Career
Chapter 4: How to Figure Out What You're Good At

- SOAR Analysis Worksheet: Identify your strengths, opportunities, aspirations, and results.

- https://www.sciencedirect.com/topics/social-sciences/soar-analysis
- LinkedIn Skills Assessment: Measure your proficiency in various skills to identify strengths. **LinkedIn**

Chapter 5: Skills That Matter (and How to Get Them)

- Coursera & edX: Free/paid courses on in-demand skills like data analysis, communication, and leadership. Coursera | Online Courses & Credentials From Top Educators. Join for Free | Build new skills. Advance your career. | edX(https://coursera.com)
- Skillshare: Learn practical skills from graphic design to project management. https://www.skillshare.com

Chapter 6: Why Making Mistakes is Part of the Plan

- TED Talk: The Gift of Failure by Jessica Lahey: A perspective on why mistakes are essential for growth.(https://www.ted.com)
- Failure Resume Guide: How to create a "failure resume" to reflect on lessons learned. https://www.failforward.org

Chapter 7: Building Confidence Without Faking It

- Confidence-Building Exercises: Tools to develop self-confidence authentically. https://www.physchologytoday.com/us/blog
- Amy Cuddy's TED Talk on Power Posing: Using body language to boost confidence. https://www.ted.com

Part 3: Landing the Job

Chapter 8: How to Write a CV That Gets Noticed

- Zety CV Builder: Easy-to-use CV templates and tips for crafting a professional CV. Zety - Professional Resume & Cover Letter Tools For Any Job(https://zety.com)
- Indeed CV Writing Guide: Step-by-step advice for building an effective resume. https://www.indeed.com/career-advice

Chapter 9: Acing the Interview

- Big Interview: Interview training platform with mock interviews and coaching. #1 Job Interview Training Platform (1,000,000+ users)(https://biginterview.com)
- The STAR Method: Framework for answering behavioural questions in interviews. How To Use the STAR Interview Response Technique | Indeed.com(https://www.indeed.com/career-advice/interviewing)

Chapter 10: Networking Without Feeling Awkward

- LinkedIn Learning: Networking Strategies: Courses to improve networking skills. **LinkedIn Learning**
- How to Network Effectively: Harvard Business Review article with actionable tips. https://hrb.org/20156/05

Part 4: Thriving in the Workplace (And Beyond)

Chapter 11: Starting Your First Job (And Doing It Well)

- Manager Tools: Offers practical tips on making a great first impression at work. Home | Manager Tools(https://www.manager-tools.com)
- Forbes: New Job Checklist: A helpful guide to starting a new role on the right foot. https://www.forbes.com

Chapter 12: Mastering Workplace Social Skills and Etiquette

- MindTools: Building Rapport in the Workplace: A guide on how to establish trust and build relationships at work. MindTools | Home(https://www.mindtools.com)
- Forbes: The Basics of Business Etiquette: Covers essential workplace etiquette, including communication, meetings, and general behaviour, providing insight into professional manners. https://www.forbes.com/sites

- The Balance Careers: How to Handle Office Politics: Practical tips on understanding and navigating office politics while maintaining professionalism. Important Computer Skills for Workplace Success

Chapter 13: How to Keep Growing in Your Career

- Skillshare Leadership Classes: Classes on leadership, communication, and team management. https://www.skillshare.com
- Udemy: Career Development Courses: Topics on career advancement and growth. Online Courses - Learn Anything, On Your Schedule | Udemy(https://www.thebalancemoney.com)

Chapter 14: Finding Balance and Avoiding Burnout

- Headspace: Meditation and mindfulness for managing stress. Meditation and Sleep Made Simple - Headspace(https://www.headspace.com)
- Harvard Business Review: Avoiding Burnout: Insights on maintaining work-life balance. 4 Steps to Beating Burnout(https://hbr.org)

Part 5: Career Change or Curveball? That's Okay Too!

Chapter 15: When You Want to Change Your Career (And Don't Know How)

- The Muse: Career Change Guide: Steps for making a career pivot successfully. https://www.themuse.com/advice/the-ultimate-guide-to-changing-careers
- LinkedIn Career Explorer: See how your skills match up with other careers. LinkedIn Career Explorer

Chapter 16: Handling Career Curveballs (And Bouncing Back)

- TED Talk: The 3 Secrets of Resilient People by Lucy Hone: Insights into resilience in the face of setbacks.(https://www.ted.com)
- Resilience Toolkit: Tools and exercises to help build resilience at work. Developing Resilience - Overcoming and Growing from

Setbacks(https://www.mindtools.com/ao310a2/developing resilience)

Chapter 17: The Future of Work:

- World Economic Forum: The Future of Jobs Report: This report offers insights into the future of work, including emerging industries, in-demand skills, and the impact of automation and AI. The Future of Jobs Report 2020 | World Economic Forum(https://www.weforum.org)

- LinkedIn Learning: Future-Proofing Your Career: Courses on adapting to changes in the workplace, staying relevant, and leveraging new technologies. **LinkedIn Learning**

- Harvard Business Review: The Skills You Need for the Future of Work: This article highlights the essential skills for thriving in the future workforce, including adaptability, emotional intelligence, and digital literacy. **HBR Skills for the Future**(https://hbr.org/2020/07)

- Coursera: The Future of Work Specialization: A series of courses exploring trends like AI, automation, and the gig economy, and how to prepare for the changing work landscape. **Coursera Future of Work**(https://www.coursera.org/specializations/future-of-work)

About the Author - Guy Ellis

I call myself an executive coach, trainer, consultant, author and lifelong learner. And I dabble in anything else that takes my interest.

I have two GenZ children who are at different stages of their careers.

My interest in careers and career planning began when I decided to immigrate to the UK, from New Zealand, at the age of 13. My ensuing school and university subject choices stemmed from that early decision.

Buying a one-way ticket, I arrived in London at the age of 21. On gaining my first permanent role at 22, I recklessly decided that I would set my sights on becoming a Human Resources Director by the time I was 32. Which I did when I was 29. Again, my career choices during my twenties were driven by that goal.

Since then, I've switched careers twice, from Human Resources to Project Management / Consultancy, and then to Coach and Trainer, and continue to believe in the power of education and being open to new opportunities as they arise.

I was lucky enough to have some insightful mentoring in my twenties which gave me the foundations for roles and careers which I have enjoyed over the last 35 years (and still counting).

I now try to repay that advice forward, recently with my good friend Graham Scott when we wrote a book on GenZ in the workplace (recently re-released by BookBoon) and mentoring young people and HR professionals.

The spark for this book came when my son, recently graduated, expressed interest in how I knew what profession I wanted to work in when I was 18. From my mentoring and coaching experience, I realised that my personal career clarity at such a young age was unusual, and given my background in coaching, careers and engaging young people in the workplace, I was uniquely placed to write this book.

If you're really interested, you can look up all of my experiences on LinkedIn. And say hello if you do.

Outside of work I love puppies, small babies and the smell of roasting chestnuts. But not usually all together.

I can be contacted at:

Personal website: https://www.guyellis.net

LinkedIn: https://www.linkedin.com/in/guy-ellis-executive-coach

Substack: https://substack.com/@guyellis1

www.ingramcontent.com/pod-product-compliance
Lightning Source LLC
Chambersburg PA
CBHW071558220526
45469CB00003B/1057